Think Better, Lead Better

Transforming Your Leadership
Through Understanding Your Brain

Jonathan Chalstrey

Contents

1. Why think better?

You're a rational, balanced leader, right? When you go to work you appraise each situation and conversation on its merits and respond in the best way to achieve your long-term objectives. You are both aware of and in control of your emotions like excitement, anxiety, joy or frustration.

Right?

Wrong!

You have a brain that is wired to appraise any situation not as a neutral observer but as someone who needs to survive and thrive. Your appraisal will contain a crucial emotional component, the purpose of which is to motivate you to act swiftly to survive or thrive[1].

You also have a brain that is wired to survive first and thrive second. So you are more responsive to a perceived threat than to an opportunity. And if you have learned a fear response to a person or a situation, you have a brain that doesn't forget it, even if it subsequently learns to recognise that fear and control it[2].

Still think you're a rational, balanced leader? It gets worse!

Your brain has a preference for categorical, well-defined perceptions and thoughts even if the information coming in to your brain is highly ambiguous[3]. This is advantageous to you if you need to do something fast, like avoid a potential threat or grasp an opportunity. It's disadvantageous to you if you need to update strongly held assumptions or inferences in response to new information or meet a new, complex challenge.

…and worse still!

Once you've made up your mind about someone and a situation you find it difficult to change your mind. When your brain is not occupied with specific problem solving activities like parking in a tight spot or checking the cost of the goods in your shopping basket, it doesn't switch off but tends to default to a neural network which creates stories or narratives about your own and other people's histories. Having created a narrative about you and another person your brain is now biased towards noticing only those new pieces of data that either confirm or strengthen that narrative[4]. Your narrative drives how you behave in subsequent conversations with that person, imposing your subjective view on the conversations and affecting the outcome of them.

The latest neuroscience research is showing us how the human brain is good at:

- Sensing danger or opportunity and motivating us to act quickly
- Thinking on 'autopilot' to conserve energy

… and not so good at:

- Thinking through today's complex business challenges in collaboration with others
- Updating strongly held beliefs in response to new information

What are the implications for leaders? We find it hard to:

- Think and act big picture and long term
- Anticipate change or respond to it
- Grasp new ideas and innovate
- Formulate sustainable solutions to challenges / problems
- Interact with others to everyone's benefit

It's almost as if the human brain has evolved for a completely different set of challenges from those that leadership right here and now presents to us. If you think and feel this way, this book will help you to have some insights to how you can think and lead better.

Or may be you believe you personally appraise each work situation and conversation in a truly objective manner based on its merits and that you are fully in control of your emotions. If that is the case I respectfully challenge you to read this book and think again in the light of the mounting evidence to the contrary from the neuroscience community. I challenge you to read this book and gain some insights to your brain, beliefs and behaviour.

This is a book about…

- Understanding why we behave the way we do when leading at work
- Gaining insights into what's really going on in our heads while leading
- Identifying how we can lead others better

What's my purpose?

I want to help leaders (including myself) to lead better, enjoy their leadership more and find more meaning in it. It is not my purpose to tell you how to do your job, lecture you on what is right and wrong, tell you how to seize your personal opportunities or solve your problems. I invite you to think of me as an extension to your brain – someone who can supply some alternative scripts or narratives for your mind to consider in order to make sense of your current leadership and spark some new approaches in your thinking which you can try for the future.

I hope that by recounting some of the most frequently expressed leadership challenges I have encountered with my individual clients during the last ten years, you will gain some insights into your own leadership. Each chapter more or less follows the following format:

1. I explore the leadership challenge that my client faced
2. I describe what the client learned from recent neuroscience and the insights it gave them into their leadership thinking and behaviour

3. I describe the tools and techniques they are using to capitalise on these insights and improve their leadership
4. They describe their experience in using these tools and techniques

I've worked with thousands of leaders over the last twelve years and the following are by far the most frequently expressed challenges they face and which are the chapter titles of this book:

- Leading change
- Motivating people
- Dealing with 'difficult' personalities
- Collaborating in teams

As they have faced up to these challenges, leaders have typically looked to sharpen their skills in areas like setting direction and goals, planning, designing and implementing work structures, processes, systems and procedures. Without a doubt this has helped but it has only got them so far. Leaders consistently report that wrestling with the above challenges involves the complex (messy) businesses of understanding themselves and their interactions with other people better.

Mind or brain?

Many of these leaders have been happy to explore the beliefs, mindsets and assumptions that drive their behaviour when leading others. In the process they have had insights to why they behave the way they do, what they could change about their leadership and how to go about making changes. They have found that understanding their minds can improve their leadership.

But to really understand our minds and improve our leadership, I believe we really need to understand our brains. Why? New information and hypotheses from neuroscientists and evolutionary biologists are influencing our understanding of human behaviour like never before. Neuroscience is contributing to new thinking about leadership in areas as diverse as visioning and creativity, problem solving and decision making, self awareness and relationship building, resilience and personal effectiveness.

The most popular psychological models that many leaders currently use to develop themselves, for example those concerning personality type, are essentially theories about how our minds work. Now we have the opportunity to test these models and theories with information about how our brains work. To what extent will the models hold up? How much utility will they continue to provide for current and future leaders? The Copernican model of the universe with the sun at the centre was beautiful and elegant and subsequently shown to be wrong by scientists using ever more powerful telescopes. The model has been consigned to the history of astronomy. Perhaps many of our current models about the human mind will go in to the history books as neuroscience and its research technologies blossom. The great opportunity here is to produce better models of how our minds work based on fresh insights from understanding how our brains work.

Neuroscience is beginning to show us that what, why and how we think is profoundly influenced by the structures and functions of our brains. While each of us possesses a unique brain, we all belong to a species of animal, homo sapiens, which has evolved a brain primed to perform many functions to help us to survive and thrive. When we become conscious of these functions we can start to understand how they influence what we do and say at work and the manner in which we think, feel, act, speak and interact with others. When we consciously understand our brains we have the potential to control, modulate and even change our thinking, feeling and behaviour and therefore our interactions with others.

Unconscious survival machines

In 'The Selfish Gene' Richard Dawkins postulates that you could regard all life forms as survival machines whose ultimate function is to transport genes through time via successive generations. In an analogous way, we could postulate that the human brain has evolved structures and functions specifically to assist each of us to survive long enough to pass on our genes to the next generation and nurture that generation sufficiently well for it to pass on the genes to the following generation. From this perspective we could regard the fact that the human brain is capable of reflective, evaluative, purposeful, conscious thought as a mere by-product of the evolutionary imperative to pass on genes. Neuroscience is now showing us that activity in the regions of the brain we use for conscious, deliberative thought represents only a small part of our total brain activity. It's showing us that much of what the human brain does has nothing to do with conscious, deliberative thought at all.

So how will understanding our brains help us to become better leaders? Let's spend some time describing what we currently know about how our brains work and an answer will start to emerge.

Effortful versus effortless

A good place to start understanding our brains is to distinguish between controlled and automatic brain processes and also between cognitive and affective processes. Camerer, Lowenstein and Prelec summarise it well. We invoke controlled processes when we encounter a challenge or surprise. Controlled processes are serial, subjectively feel like they require effort and we can give a good introspective account of them. For example, if I asked you how you solved a maths problem or how you chose your new mobile device, it is likely that you will recall the considerations and the steps leading to your solution or choice. In contrast, automatic brain processes operate in parallel, are not so accessible to consciousness, and are relatively effortless. When brain processes operate in parallel they facilitate rapid response and multitasking. This gives the brain remarkable power when it comes to certain types of tasks, for example visual identification or language processing. Since automatic processes are not so accessible to consciousness, we often have surprisingly little introspective insight into why our brains made automatic choices or judgements. We perceive a face as "trustworthy" or a verbal remark as "aggressive" automatically and apparently effortlessly[5].

We also have cognitive and affective processes running in our brains – thinking and feeling processes would be a useful short hand. It seems counter intuitive but most affective (feeling) processes operate outside conscious awareness only entering our consciousness when they reach a threshold of intensity. These affective processes are motivating us either to avoid or approach people or situations before we are even aware of it. Cognitive processes, in contrast, help us to answer true/false questions.

Camerer, Lowenstein and Prelec summarise this information about brain processes into a model to which I have added representative box names and some day-to-day examples of those brain processes in action.

Brain Processes	Cognitive (Thinking) Purpose: True or false	Affective (Feeling) Purpose: Avoid or approach
Controlled • serial • effortful • evoked deliberately • good introspective access	J U D G E e.g. How I chose my new mobile phone Solving 17 x 24	F R I E N D e.g. Crying while watching an ad for a cancer charity Feeling inspired by her enthusiastic perspective
Automatic • parallel • effortless • reflexive • poor introspective access	A U T O P I L O T e.g. Driving my familiar route to work Operating a familiar work process	A N I M A L e.g. BOO! Response She grimaced and is a threat He looks trustworthy

What practical use is there for you as a leader in understanding brain processes? Please indulge me with your attention a little longer and I hope you will be able to construct your own useful answer.

Let's illustrate the model with a common work scenario (with apologies to Camerer *et al* for appropriating, tweaking and then extrapolating from their example). You're attending a meeting of colleagues from across different departments of your organisation. As you take a seat, the person chairing the meeting approaches you with a plate of biscuits inviting you to take one.

AUTOPILOT: The first task for your brain is to figure out what is on the plate. The occipital cortex in the back of the brain is the first on the scene, drawing in signals from your eyes via your optic nerves. It decodes the biscuits into primitive shapes such as lines and corners then uses a "cascading process" to discern larger shapes. Further downstream, in the inferior temporal cortex, this information becomes integrated with stored representations of objects, which permits you to recognise the objects on the plate as biscuits.

ANIMAL: This is where affect enters the picture. Outputs of the inferior temporal visual cortex as well as outputs from other sensory systems feed into the orbitofrontal cortex to determine the threat or reward value of the recognised object. This is a highly particular representation. What is represented is neither pure information (i.e. that these are biscuits) nor pure utility (i.e. that is something I like) but rather a fusion of information *and* utility. It is as if certain neurons in the orbitofrontal cortex are saying "These are biscuits and I want them."

The reward value of biscuits depends in turn on many factors. First, there is your personal history with biscuits. If you pigged out on biscuits to the point of feeling sick in the past, you may have learned an unconscious and automatic aversion to them. The amygdala seems to play a critical role in this kind of long-term learning. Secondly, the reward value of the biscuits will depend on your current level of hunger. The orbitofrontal cortex and subcortical region called the hypothalamus are sensitive to your level of hunger. Neurons in these regions fire more rapidly at the sight or taste of food when you are hungry, and fire less rapidly when you are not hungry.

JUDGE and FRIEND: Processing often ends before these types of brain processes go to work. If you are hungry, and like biscuits, your motor cortex will guide your arm to reach for a biscuit and eat it, drawing on automatic boxes AUTOPILOT (reaching) and ANIMAL (taste and enjoyment) processes. However, higher level processing might also now come on line. For example, if you recently read an article on the health risks of eating high sugar food items, you may recoil; or if you dislike biscuits but anticipate disappointment in the eyes of the meeting Chair who bought the biscuits herself, you'll eat it anyway (or pick it up and discreetly hide it under your papers when she turns to serve other guests). These explicit thoughts JUDGE and FRIEND involve anticipated feelings (your own and the Chair's) and draw on explicit memories from the hippocampus, inputs from the affect system and anticipation from the prefrontal cortex.

Let's pause. We're starting to get a picture of how controlled and automatic, cognitive and affective processes work together in the human brain. But I suspect you're thinking something like "But how is this of any practical use to me as a leader?" Let's illustrate the model with a second work scenario that might elicit some more practical insights. You're attending a meeting of colleagues from across different departments of your organisation. As you sit down the meeting Chair makes eye contact with you and for a microsecond she clearly grimaces.

AUTOPILOT: The occipital cortex is the first on the scene, enabling you to recognise that you are looking at a face and more specifically the face of the Chair.

ANIMAL: This is where affect enters the picture. Outputs of the inferior temporal visual cortex as well as outputs from other sensory systems feed into the orbitofrontal cortex to determine the threat or reward value of the recognised object. You match the grimace to that signifying an angry face. What is represented is a fusion of information *and* utility "This is the Chair and she's a threat."

The threat value of the Chair depends in turn on many factors. One important factor here is your personal history with her. If you recently had a series of arguments you may have an unconscious and automatic aversion to her. The amygdala seems to play a critical role in this kind of long-term learning.

JUDGE and FRIEND: Processing often ends before these types of brain processes go to work. If you are fearful your motor cortex will guide your feet to a seat away from the gaze of the Chair, drawing on AUTOPILOT (walking and sitting) and ANIMAL (submission) processes. However, higher level processing might also now come on line JUDGE and FRIEND. For example, if you know that the Chair is having a particularly tough time fending off a hostile takeover bid for the business and you can empathise with her predicament, you might think that the grimace is somehow connected to the current stress levels in her life and not specifically aimed at you. You might therefore choose to make and hold eye contact with her and say "Hi" in a friendly, reassuring way. You have used these explicit, conscious thoughts to reappraise the situation and choose how you will act.

Or, using another high level processing approach JUDGE you might focus on the present moment sensations you are experiencing as you sit down for this meeting. You might question: how does my body feel right now? Is there a sudden tightness in my grip on the papers I am holding, or in my chest as I breathe? Are my thoughts beginning to race, pulling me to replay and dissect my recent history with the Chair so I can make some sort of sense of my current discomfort? Can I be curious about what I am experiencing, simply accept that I am experiencing it without a negative judgement on myself or the Chair and leave it in the past[6]?

Doing either of the above higher level processing activities (reappraisal and mindfulness) could impact very positively on how you behaved subsequently in the meeting. For example, if you needed to challenge something the Chair contributed during the meeting in a positive rather than negative way or really probe through questioning her perspective on a particular issue in an assertive but non-confrontational manner. Both of these would be fine examples of in-the-moment leadership behaviour.

I hope you are beginning to appreciate some practical utility in understanding how your brain works and its impact on your leadership behaviours.

Thinking better in critical leadership conversations

Achieving a greater understanding of your brain processes could open up all sorts of possibilities for your leadership by helping you to analyse better what's really going on in a leadership conversation or situation. For example, you might get an insight to:

- Why you have perceived a person or situation in a particular way
- How you could perceive that situation or conversation differently
- A different behaviour you could deploy and a different outcome to a conversation or situation that might follow from that different behaviour

You might also become eager to learn about techniques that might make you more consciously aware of currently unconscious cognitive or affective processes in your brain so that you could better answer questions like:

- How am I currently thinking about a particular conversation or situation? What are different ways of thinking about this conversation or situation?

- How am I currently feeling about a particular conversation or situation? What are different ways of feeling about this conversation or situation?

And why would you want to think or feel differently about a conversation or situation? Well it might just give you more choices of action to influence how the conversation or situation develops and its eventual outcome.

OK, reality check. So may be you're thinking right now that there might be something in this neuroscience stuff that might enlighten your leadership somewhere along the way. "But surely (you may be thinking) we've evolved a brain that's best able to get us through the days, months and years, so why do we really need to analyse how it works and understand it?" After all, you don't need to know how a car works to use it to get from A to B. However, here is where I invoke both my experience as a leadership coach and practitioner over the last twelve years as well as my personal life experience to date of over fifty years. I've witnessed leaders (including myself) say and do the right thing in nine out of ten situations, maybe in ninety nine out of a hundred situations, but on the one critical occasion when the conversation or situation is new, the stakes are high and there's a lot riding on the outcome, they get it wrong. This is not because they're bad or negligent but because they are using old ways of thinking to deal with a new situation.

What if you could deal with that new, critical leadership conversation or situation (that you might well have today) and increase your chances of getting it right?

What if you could…

…consciously identify the automatic affective brain processes that have been triggered to appraise this new situation and be aware of your current feeling (i.e. JUDGE becomes aware of ANIMAL)

…consciously identify the automatic cognitive processes you are using to appraise this new situation and be aware of your traditional thinking (i.e. JUDGE becomes aware of AUTOPILOT)

…consciously simulate the feelings of another person involved in this new situation in order to inform your conscious reflection, evaluation and decision making (i.e. FRIEND informs JUDGE)

… be mindful of your feelings and thoughts in response to this new situation and deliberately reappraise it (i.e. JUDGE controls ANIMAL and AUTOPILOT)

…practice new behaviours to deal with this type of situation until they become unconscious, effortless habit (i.e. effortful JUDGE thinking becomes new, effortless AUTOPILOT thinking)?

Maybe an example might help here.

You've just finished an exhausting project planning meeting and as you sit on the train back to the office you scan email on your phone. You notice one from your colleague Sally to a client, copied to you, with an attached proposal which you drafted yesterday and to which Sally agreed to add a paragraph about her own area before sending on to the client today. You open the proposal and with rising alarm you notice that Sally has significantly changed the structure of your draft. You feel threatened (ANIMAL) and a strong need to do something about it immediately. You call Sally but it goes to voice mail. This raises your feeling of threat even more.

As your train journey continues, you start reflecting on why Sally would restructure the proposal without consulting you first and certainly before sending it to the client. Last week she interrupted you in a meeting to steer the discussion in a different direction which annoyed you. Yesterday, she didn't like the format of your report to the board and suggested lots of changes, some of which seemed petty. Now she's changed your draft of a client proposal, replacing a structure which you and colleagues across the organisation agreed a number of years ago and which everyone uses. You conclude that this is just another example of her controlling behaviour. By the time you've got back to the office your ruminations have prepared you for a fight with Sally.

As you walk in the office, Sally looks up and some part of you responds positively to her genuine smile and 'hello' (ANIMAL). You ask "How did the board presentation go?" She replies, "OK, no nightmare moments I'm pleased to say!.. and thanks for your input." You feel comfortable enough to ask "I notice you restructured the proposal for Stokers (the client). Why did you do that?" (JUDGE). She replies, "Yes I did. I got your draft for me to add my bits to and was pretty much done with it when Alan from Stokers called in a bit of a panic. He said he was presenting our proposal to his senior colleagues this afternoon and had only just seen the criteria for supplier selection that his colleagues were going to use to judge our proposal. Since he really wants us to be successful with this bid, he told me there and then how we needed to structure our proposal and I edited your draft accordingly. I wanted to call you to discuss but when I checked your calendar I noticed you were already in your project planning meeting and Alan needed our submission within the hour to prepare for his own meeting."

While you're aware that you still have a lingering feeling of threat and a desire to fight, Sally's explanation rings true. Alan is a great ally at Stokers but badly organised and with a tendency to create a drama. You accept Sally's explanation (i.e. JUDGE controls ANIMAL). You would have done the same in her situation (i.e. FRIEND informs JUDGE) and you start to feel more comfortable.

You start imagining what it felt like for Sally today in front of the board. You know from experience what a grilling they can give senior executives like Sally and you. You recall that next week she will have to update the board on the project planning meeting from which you've just come.

You are reminded of the anxiety you were feeling about the extra work you have just taken on as a result of the project planning meeting (JUDGE becomes aware of ANIMAL). But you simultaneously reflect on how motivated Sally feels about this project and how willing she is to support and even champion you to the board. (i.e. more FRIEND informs JUDGE).

You identify both feelings of frustration and slight panic at the work to be done but remind yourself that the work is on a project with which you really want to be involved and start to feel calmer. It's a worthwhile project and you're working with good people. (i.e. JUDGE controls ANIMAL) and worth the effort of the extra work. You block 15 minutes out of your diary to plan how you will tackle the extra work for the project. It takes effort to focus your mind on the many aspects but a structured approach starts to emerge (JUDGE).

The following week as you leave the next project meeting there is part of you that is already thinking constructively about what else needs to be done to keep the project on track using the structured approach you've already thought through (i.e. effortful JUDGE thinking becomes new, effortless AUTOPILOT thinking).

For better or worse

Every leadership situation presents us with the possibility of thinking and leading better or worse than before. Viewed through the lens of our brain processes model, here's how our thinking in a new leadership situation could make us act more effectively.

Think better, lead better

Brain Processes	Cognitive (Thinking) Purpose: True or false	Affective (Feeling) Purpose: Avoid or approach
Controlled • serial • effortful • evoked deliberately • good introspective access	J U D G E I hold different sets of information, different views or perspectives in mind long enough to make meaningful comparisons, evaluate them and come to better judgements and decisions	F R I E N D I empathise with how others think and feel to understand a situation much better
Automatic • parallel • effortless • reflexive • poor introspective access	A U T O P I L O T I recognise correctly the situations where I can use tried and tested assumptions and mindsets	A N I M A L My unconscious impressions and intuitions alert me to threats or opportunities which I consciously check out to see how real they are

In contrast, here's how our thinking in a new leadership situation could make us act ineffectively.

Think worse, lead worse

Brain Processes	Cognitive (Thinking) Purpose: True or false	Affective (Feeling) Purpose: Avoid or approach
Controlled • serial • effortful • evoked deliberately • good introspective access	J U D G E e.g. My conscious thinking is so objective that it no longer takes account of my subjective values, beliefs or personal motivations	F R I E N D e.g. I empathise with others to such an extent that I lose my objectivity
Automatic • parallel • effortless • reflexive • poor introspective access	A U T O P I L O T e.g. I operate from unconscious, tried and tested assumptions or mindsets which are no longer of use in the situation I find myself	A N I M A L e.g. My unconscious impressions and intuitions drive my conscious thinking and decision making in the wrong direction

Leading change

In order to gain insights to our own leadership thinking, feeling and action, it really helps to analyse and critique other leaders' situations. We often learn much by drawing analogies between others' situations and our own. With this in mind much of this book shares the challenges, thinking, feeling and actions of leaders I have had the privilege and pleasure to coach in recent years. While the leaders and their conversations I describe in this book are fictional, they are based on information I have gathered from real coaching conversations I have had with my clients. This means you can eavesdrop on some real leadership experiences while the anonymity of the leaders is protected.

In chapter two you will read about Richard whose challenge was to influence his management team to initiate a major change. Richard heads a directorate at a UK public sector institution with several hundred staff.

Before I met Richard he had transformed his directorate over an eight-year period from an average performer to one with the highest government quality rating in the UK. No mean achievement! He had done this by having a clear vision of where the directorate should focus its interests and resources. He had also plugged the directorate into the key government initiatives of the day. He had introduced logical and robust systems and procedures.

As he personally prepared to move to an even more senior role in the organisation he knew that if his legacy at the directorate was to be sustained he needed to develop his management team to take it forward without him.

Specifically, he wanted to introduce a performance management process that would promote excellence throughout all echelons. He wanted the new process to deliver better…

- Strategic thinkers – with a clear vision for the future and the actions required to make the vision reality

- Conceptual thinkers – who are aware of what is occurring in the world in order to generate more creative and imaginative solutions to problems and issues

- Drivers for excellence – people who would strive personally and with their teams to identify and implement fresh, innovative ways of doing things

- Strategic influencers – formulaters of long-term change initiatives who could use different influencing strategies to win commitment from others

Richard set about introducing his new performance management process with his customary energy and gusto. Initially he was met with a polite, passing interest from his line managers, as if this were merely a topic for casual debate. As he pressed on, more and more of his management staff actively resisted his exhortations for them to use the new process to appraise their own staff or be appraised themselves. The responses behind Richard's back ranged from…

'Well of course we do all this stuff already so it's just going to be an additional administrative burden for people to provide evidence that they are actually doing it."

…to…

"My line report staff really are very bright and capable people but once they've done the day job there just isn't time for this more strategic, forward-looking work."

…to..

"All this stuff which Richard wants is beyond my pay grade. It's for the leadership level above me and ultimately Richard's responsibility, not mine."

Richard was failing to influence his management team to engage with the new process and the staff development it implied. He had initiated other major change initiatives before and faced similar resistance. As Richard said "I know it's a cliché, Jonathan, but at times it really has felt like wading through treacle!" In those earlier situations he had finally used his line authority to impose change – prescribing what his managers would do differently and how. He was at the same point of forcing through the introduction of the new process when he paused. Why? When he had imposed change in the past most of his managers had complied and gone along with it. A few had openly rebelled and caused painful ructions. Some had nodded assent to Richard's face but tried to undermine the change behind his back. Only a few managers had been truly committed to the change, engaging with it fully, being creative and innovative with its introduction and successfully gaining commitment from their staff. Most had just gone along for the ride for an easy life. Consequently Richard had found himself constantly pushing for progress to be made, constantly monitoring what was going on, nagging or hectoring his management team.

Richard couldn't help but wonder whether his change initiatives would be sustained if he were no longer there to push them forward when he had moved on. He wanted the introduction of a new performance management process to be different from the other change initiatives he had undertaken.

What could he learn from neuroscience that might help him understand the art of influencing his colleagues better? What could he learn from studies of the brain activity of effective influencers who are expert at taking the perspective of others and with that perspective formulate strategies for shifting the thinking of others[7]? What tools and techniques might help him to emulate the behaviours of these effective influencers and win more people over to his new performance management process and the staff development at its heart? In terms of our brain processes model, how could he fire up FRIEND in order to inform JUDGE? We'll examine his story in detail in chapter two.

Motivating people

Imagine a stocky man in his 30s who speaks English in a strident manner with a strong Russian accent and who manages project teams in an international bank. You're now imagining Vladimir. Here's a rough transcript from a coaching conversation I had with him:

"Jonathan, I have a colleague who is only motivated by promotion but I do not have the power to promote him. So what can I do?"

"OK Vladimir, what leads you to believe that your colleague is only motivated by promotion?"

"When you have worked in the bank for two years you should expect a promotion or your career is going nowhere and he has been with the bank now for more than two years."

"OK, what is it about a promotion that you think motivates your colleague?"

"I don't know I never asked him."

"OK, so may be you could ask him. But for now, just try and put yourself in his shoes. What is it about a promotion that you think motivates your colleague?"

"The extra pay and the better job title."

"Yes, for sure. For how long after the promotion do you think the extra pay and the better job title will motivate your colleague to do the best job he can?"

"Hmmm….I don't know….may be a few weeks or months."

"OK, so let's just imagine your colleague gets his promotion and a few months have gone by and he is no longer motivated by the extra pay and better job title. What's going to re-motivate him?"

"Another promotion!"

(We both laugh)

"OK, so let's assume that we can't keep promoting your colleague every few months to motivate him otherwise he would be CEO in a year! What is it about a promotion other than extra pay and better job title that you think motivates your colleague?"

(Vladimir pauses before he replies)

"Well, the promotion is recognition of the work he has already done….the effort he has already made. It shows the bank thinks he is important."

"How could the bank show it thinks your colleague is important other than promoting him?

"The bank could involve him in high profile projects where he gets to work with important stakeholders and he has significant responsibilities."

"Who in the bank has the power to involve your colleague in high profile projects where he gets to work with important stakeholders and he has significant responsibilities?"

"Well lots of people…..I guess I sometimes have that power too."

As Vladimir and I continued the conversation I got the feeling that he was beginning to become aware that he was operating from a limiting assumption that his colleague was only motivated by a promotion and to think about challenging that assumption.

As we continued with the coaching conversation we started to explore what really motivates people at work and in particular the AUTOPILOT and ANIMAL brain processes involved. We explored how:

- We tend to perceive threats more readily than opportunities[3]
- We learn patterns of thinking which can automatically generate fear or anxiety

- However, we also have the thinking capacity (JUD(processes) to recognise how fear or anxiety is motiv to inappropriate and negative actions
- We have the capacity to 'overwrite' negative thought patterns[4]
- Our own behaviour as leaders can either create fear in others or positive emotions

Next we explored how we could use more positive thinking, feeling and actions to motivate people to exceptional performance. We explored how we can:

1. Use purpose to gain commitment
2. Encourage autonomy to gain innovation
3. Encourage mastery to gain high quality
4. Facilitate connection to gain discretionary effort (or going the extra mile)

What insights did this give Vladimir into his own motivation as a leader and the motivation of the members of his team? You can find out more in chapter three.

Dealing with 'difficult' personalities

One of the most frequent moans I hear from leaders was summarised by one of my clients called Stella. She said, "You know, my job would be so much easier if I didn't have such difficult personalities in the senior management team. I suppose you can't change people's personalities, can you? So I'll just have to put up with them!" Interestingly, at the beginning of our coaching sessions Stella was firmly of the view "I'm not an emotional person at work and I don't really get into conflict with people." I have heard this from leaders over the years many, many times and in most cases it turns out to be an untrue analysis even though I don't doubt that these leaders sincerely hold this view about themselves. Sometimes what these leaders mean is that they do not show emotion at work. For example, they have learned not to show anxiety or anger with colleagues even though they are experiencing one or both of these emotions internally. At other times these leaders are simply not consciously aware that they have been experiencing an emotion but through reflection in a coaching conversation it becomes plain to them that they have been (i.e. JUDGE becomes aware of ANIMAL).

When I invited Stella to question her *"You know, my job would be so much easier if I didn't have such difficult personalities in the senior management team."* narrative she ended up telling me something very, very different which seemed insightful. She said, "There are particular people in the senior management team who say and do things which trigger thoughts and emotions in me which make me behave in ways I do not want to behave and in ways I did not intend……. If I had more control over my thoughts and emotions I would not behave in these ways."

In chapter four, we'll follow Stella's story about the emotion of fear in the work place. This is not an obvious story about bullying, intimidation or victimisation. Stella is a confident and capable senior manager in a media company. She is professionally qualified and has a vast reservoir of technical skills and expertise. She is personable and has great social skills and in spite of these she has found it very difficult to challenge colleagues in senior management team meetings and some individuals in particular.

Stella and I explored some of the latest neuroscience about how the brain learns fear responses, how to recognise them as they are starting to happen and how to fire up a part of the brain which can control and dampen down the fear response[9] so that we can say what we want to say in a way that enables other people to hear and engage with it.

In chapter four, we'll explore what Stella feels in those senior management team meetings and what techniques she is employing to regulate her emotions, change her behaviour and speak up and what results that has produced. Specifically, we will explore how effective leaders:

1. Recognise that the true difficulty lies not in the personality of the other person but in their own current thinking, feeling and actions and that they can change these
2. Seek to become more consciously aware of how they are appraising a conversation or situation in terms of threat or reward and the narrative they are creating
3. Identify and regulate their emotions
4. Virtually simulate others' experiences in their minds to empathise better
5. Actively build relationships by seeking common ground first and exploring differences second

Collaborating in teams

Think about it. All the essentials of life you need as a member of a properly functioning modern, developed human society are provided by specialist groups of people. Mostly, you don't personally need to worry about protecting yourself from other humans (or animals) because we have an army, police and prison service to do that. You don't need to design, build and maintain your own house because we have architects, builders, plumbers, electricians etc. to do that. You don't need to forage or hunt for food and drink because we have farmers, logistics companies, and retailers to produce, distribute and sell food to us. We have utility companies to provide us with light and heat and we have hospitals and schools to keep us healthy and teach our children. Groups of fellow humans beings specialise in providing all these goods and services so that we personally don't have to and we can get on with something else. All you and I need to do is to earn enough money to pay for it all!

Much of what distinguishes human from other animal societies relies on the superior ability of groups of humans to work together to:

- Provide these specialist goods and services
- Lead the organisations which provide them

However, the ecological, economic, social, political, technological, commercial and legal environments in which we live are constantly changing. So one of the most important challenges for any current human organisation is how to get the teams that deliver its services and its leadership team to collaborate in the most effective manner so the organisation can survive and thrive in a changing environment.

In chapter five we'll meet Laura who is a talented senior operations manager at a leading international charity. Laura had a double challenge. First, as the newly appointed head of operations she needed to get two, newly-merged operational teams to work more effectively together. Secondly, she had recently joined a leadership team of departmental heads tasked with finding ways of working more efficiently and synergistically across departments.

Some of the issues which Laura's operational team faced included:

- Team conversations had hitherto focused on differences and there was a need to find common ground

- Some team members were ignorant or suspicious of others' experience, expertise or intent or hadn't shared information critical to the success of finding efficiencies and increased effectiveness

- Some team members' reasoning and intent needed to be more explicit for trust to grow and more honest conversations to happen

- A small group within the wider team tended to dominate conversations and prevents contributions, creativity and commitment from other team members

Interestingly, the heads of department team faced some similar issues.

Three months in to the job and Laura was beginning to feel the pressure as her operational team appeared to be falling apart before it had even really properly formed. So we spent time together

exploring how both effective leaders and effective members c
at any level of seniority in an organisation:

1. Create common cause and a sense of belonging
2. Encourage diverse and innovative thinking
3. Facilitate productive discussion and decision making

We explored what brain-friendly techniques she could use to
increase bonding between team members, particularly focusing on
creating common cause between them. We looked at how a group of
brains could be encouraged to work collaboratively to outperform
just one brain when meeting a complex business challenge.

How to use the rest of this book

Feel free to dip into any of the following chapters of this book that
interest you most before reading the rest. I invite you to follow the
narrative about the leadership situations of my coachees and how
they unfold. Why? Because that way you follow their thinking and
feeling processes as they encounter new information and gain new
insights. We know that the more you are engaged in someone else's
story and the insights you can draw for your own situation, the more
likely you are to recall those insights at the right time and act upon
them[11]. I have deliberately scattered exercises throughout each
chapter to encourage you to apply any insights you may have from
my coachees' experiences to your own situations. I am genuinely
interested in your feedback on how well these exercises work for
you and how they could be improved. I welcome a dialogue.

An alternative is to read from here to the end of the book and make
more learning connections across the whole text. The choice is
yours. I hope you enjoy and learn something. I hope you find ways
of making your leadership less effortful or more effortless and learn
to think better and lead better.

More reading?

If you want to gain more insights to the interactions between
automatic and controlled, cognitive and affective brain processes, I

would recommend you read Daniel Kahneman[12] on thinking fast and slow, Walter Mischel[13] describing hot and cold thinking or Steve Peters[14] describing a model of brain processes using the metaphors of chimp, human and computer.

Notes:

1. An Integrative Neuroscience Platform: Application to Profiles of Negativity and Positivity Bias, E. Gordon and L. Williams, Journal of Integrative Neuroscience, Volume 7, Issue 3, September 2008. Also, Neuroception: A Subconscious System for Detecting Threats and Safety. S.W. Porges, Zero to Three: Bulletin of the National Center for Infants, Toddlers and Families, 2003

2. Neural Mechanisms of Extinction Learning and Retrieval, Gregory J Quirk and Devin Mueller, Neuropsychopharmacology, 33, 56–72, 2008. Also, The Neural Bases of Attitudes, Emily B.C. Falk, Matthew D. Lieberman, from The Neural Basis of Human Belief Systems, 71-94, 2013. Also, Cognitive Neuroscience of Emotional Memory, Kevin S LaBar and Roberto Cabeza, Nature Reviews Neuroscience 7, 54-64, 2006. Also, The Emotional Brain: The Mysterious Underpinnings of Emotional Life, Joseph E.LeDoux, 1998

3. Neuroeconomics: How Neuroscience Can Inform Economics, Colin Camerer, George Lowenstein, and Drazen Prelec, Journal of Economic Literature, Vol. XLIII, 9–64, 2005

4. Attending to the Present: Mindfulness Meditation Reveals Distinct Neural Modes of Self-reference, N.A.S Farb, Z.V. Segal, H. Mayberg, J. Bean, D. McKeon, Z. Fatima, and A.K. Anderson, Social Cognitive and Affective Neuroscience, 2(4),313-122, 2007

5. Amygdala Responsivity to High-Level Social Information from Unseen Faces, Jonathan B. Freeman, Ryan M. Stolier, Zachary A. Ingbretsen and Eric A. Hehman , The Journal of Neuroscience, 34(32), 2014

6. The Mindful Brain and Emotion Regulation in Mood Disorders, Norman A. S. Farb, Adam K. Anderson and Zindel V. Segal, Can J Psychiatry, 57(2): 70–77, 2012

7. Creating Buzz: The Neural Correlates of Effective Message Propagation, Emily B. Falk, Sylvia A. Morelli, B. Locke Welborn, Karl Dambacher and Matthew D. Lieberman, Psychological Science, 24:1234, 2013

8. Social Neuroscience and Health: Neuropsychological Mechanisms Linking Social Ties with Physical Health, N.I. Eisenberger and S.W. Cole, Nature Neuroscience, 15(5):669-74, 2012

9. Intentional and Incidental Self-Control in Ventrolateral PFC, J.R. Cohen, E.T. Berkman, M.D. Lieberman In D. T. Stuss & R. T. Knight (Eds.) Principles of Frontal Lobe Function, 2nd ed., 417-440, 2013. Also, Self-Control, Y.Trope, R. Hassin and K.N. Ochsner, 2010

10. Social effects of oxytocin in humans: context and person matter, Jennifer A. Bartz, Jamil Zaki, Niall Bolger and Kevin N. Ochsner, Trends in Cognitive Sciences 15:301-309. Also, Neural Correlates of Giving Support to a Loved One, T.K. Inagaki and N.I. Eisenberger, Psychosomatic Medicine, 74(1):3-7, 2008

11. Neuroscience and Adult Learning, Louis Cozolino and Susan Sprokay, New Directions for Adult and Continuing Education, 110, summer 2006

12. Thinking Fast and Slow, Daniel Kahneman, 2011

13. The Marshmallow Test, Mastering Self-Control, Walter Mischel, 2014

14. The Chimp Paradox, Steve Peters, 2012

2. Leading Change

Do you remember Richard from Chapter 1? He was one of my clients trying to introduce a new performance management process in his directorate at a UK public sector institution with several hundred staff. Richard wasn't getting the 'buy in' from his management team that he wanted. "A lot of the time they just don't get it!" he would say to me.

Richard chose to talk with me about how to lead this change better. During the course of our conversations, I shared with him my observation that really effective leaders of change do a number of crucial things. They:

1. Challenge their own and others' beliefs about what is possible
2. Evaluate an idea for change from other people's perspectives so they can influence better
3. Use stories about characters who have aspirations and dilemmas with which their followers can identify in order to motivate people to action
4. Use informal networks to spread new ideas, behaviours and ways of doing things

We discussed each of these topics to see what light they might shed on Richard's desire to introduce a new performance management process.

Challenging beliefs

I kicked off with Richard by sharing some recent neuroscience about neural networks, thinking and the formation of beliefs, which I share with you now.

We use a neural network, which some scientists have named the *narrative neural network,* in order to create narratives we hold about our own and other people's histories. Interestingly, we don't really choose to use this network. It might be more accurate to say that we occasionally choose not to use it. We default to it when we stop using other neural networks for thinking, for example, problem-solving tasks like operating our new mobile device for the first time or completing a new budget spreadsheet[1].

The *narrative neural network* involves the medial prefrontal cortex that 'lights up' when we are considering and evaluating, plus the hippocampus that is fundamental to organising our memories. When we create a narrative we prioritise certain data over other data thereby creating meaning or making sense of the welter of random data that we see, hear, smell, taste or touch in any moment. When a narrative becomes very strong in our minds we call it a belief whose function is to guide our actions. In the context of leadership, a belief can either limit or enable our choice of actions.

When we are conscious of the narratives we create we are operating JUDGE brain processes. When these narratives are out of consciousness, for example, when we operate from automatic beliefs or assumptions, we are operating from AUTOPILOT. In contrast, we also use a neural network named the *direct experience neural network* that operates when we experience information coming into our senses in real time. This network involves the anterior cingulate cortex that helps us to notice errors and changes and switch our attention, plus the insula that helps us to perceive our own bodily sensations. We could describe this as JUDGE consciousness being very open to AUTOPILOT and ANIMAL brain processes.

Brain Processes	Cognitive (Thinking) Purpose: True or false	Affective (Feeling) Purpose: Avoid or approach
Controlled • serial • effortful • evoked deliberately • good introspective access	J U D G E	F R I E N D
Automatic • parallel • effortless • reflexive • poor introspective access	A U T O P I L O T	A N I M A L

The *narrative neural network* and the *direct experience neural network* are inversely correlated so when one is more active the other is less active. So what? When we are occupied in creating narratives we become less good at noticing what's going on around us and less aware of our feelings in response.

What has this to do with leading change? If we're going to challenge existing strongly held beliefs about what is possible in respect of leading a particular change, we need to be able to challenge our narrative with new data and revise the narrative so it moves from limiting to increasing our potential actions. Firing up our *direct experience neural network* can provide us with that new data. With new data we can have new insights and understand people, situations, threats and opportunities in new ways.

For better or worse

Viewed through the lens of our brain processes model, here's how our thinking about leading change could make us act more effectively.

Think better, lead change better

Brain Processes	Cognitive (Thinking) Purpose: True or false	Affective (Feeling) Purpose: Avoid or approach
Controlled • serial • effortful • evoked deliberately • good introspective access	J U D G E e.g. Assemble the facts and figures about the proposed change to: Be clear why the change is necessary, the big picture and long-term benefits Agree clear goals Present a plausible plan for discussion	F R I E N D e.g. Take others' perspectives on the proposed change to: Understand more fully benefits and disadvantages Influence others to support Deal with their objections
Automatic • parallel • effortless • reflexive • poor introspective access	A U T O P I L O T e.g. Draw on existing positive mindsets about: The value of change When it's worked out well in the past Involving others to make it happen	A N I M A L e.g. Check out impressions and intuitions about how people are perceiving and judging the proposed change

In contrast, here's how our thinking about leading change could make us act less effectively.

Think worse, lead change worse

Brain Processes	Cognitive (Thinking) Purpose: True or false	Affective (Feeling) Purpose: Avoid or approach
Controlled • serial • effortful • evoked deliberately • good introspective access	J U D G E e.g. Assemble an objective and rational case and plan for the change that looks great in theory but which does not take account of people's real experiences	F R I E N D e.g. Over empathise with opponents of change to the point of colluding with them and sabotaging the change
Automatic • parallel • effortless • reflexive • poor introspective access	A U T O P I L O T e.g. Operate from limiting assumptions about: Why change needs to happen What needs to change How it can be achieved	A N I M A L e.g. Be spooked by negative impressions and intuitions about how people are perceiving and judging the proposed change and back off

How could Richard think better to lead the change he wanted? What beliefs was he holding about why and how best to introduce a new performance management process? If he could become aware of those beliefs, could he also consider to what extent those beliefs were either limiting or enabling his choice of leadership actions? How could he fire up his *direct experience* neural *network* to increase his awareness of what was going on around him at work? How could he gather the data he needed to create a deeper understanding of the possibilities and challenges of introducing a new performance management process?

Here's how we set about raising Richard's self and social awareness. We applied some techniques that encouraged Richard to become aware of and challenge his current perspective. I invited Richard to try the following exercises that you can try yourself. The exercises work best if you have a particular change in mind that you want to initiate now or in the near future.

Exercise 1 – Self awareness and beliefs

To what extent do you agree with the following statements? What real-world examples support your view?

   a. People are persuaded by objective and rational facts and figures
   b. To influence others I need clarity about what I think and feel about a proposal
   c. You have to influence people at the top of a team to achieve your objectives

What sort of actions might a leader pursue to initiate change who strongly believes the above?

Now consider, what sort of actions might a leader pursue to initiate change who strongly believes the following?

   a. People are moved by and remember stories with characters with whom they can connect

b. To influence others I need clarity about what they think and feel about a proposal

c. People are mostly influenced through their informal networks of friends and colleagues

In respect of the change you want to initiate:

- What beliefs are enabling and which limiting your choices of action? Specifically, which actions are your beliefs enabling and which actions are they limiting?

- What do you want to do more of? What do you want to do less of?

Richard reported that his approach to persuading his colleagues to support and implement a new performance management process had focused on the need for objective standards of behaviour in the workplace. He had provided large amounts of objective evidence of how performance management processes that focused on behaviours had improved individual and business performance in other organisations. He had not enquired into his colleagues' thinking or feeling about the proposed change, to what extent they saw it as a threat or an opportunity.

He also reported believing that clarity and direction in the form of a detailed plan on how to implement the new process was what his colleagues wanted, or rather that's what he would want if he were them. (He had put them in his shoes rather than putting himself in their shoes.) He believed that leadership was about setting a direction and providing a detailed action plan. I wanted Richard to consider challenging this narrative he held about leading his colleagues. Why? Because I suspected it might be limiting his options. I wondered what might be the exact opposite belief he had just expressed. Richard accepted this as a purely intellectual challenge and ventured the following. Leadership is about canvassing others about a direction and challenging them to come up with a detailed plan themselves. Did he believe it? No.

I asked Richard what actions his current belief about leadership encouraged him to take. He showed me the fifty point action plans he had devised for each of his senior managers and revealed his expectation that they would have fifty point action plans for each of their direct reports and so forth down the hierarchy. He said that he had frequent one-to-one meetings with his senior managers where they would review progress methodically against each of the fifty points. He mentioned in passing that he found such meetings laborious and irritating when action points could not be ticked off.

I asked Richard if he was curious to consider what actions a leader might take who believed that leadership is about canvassing others about a direction and challenging them to come up with a detailed plan themselves. He repeated that he didn't believe it himself but was willing to consider how a leader might behave who did. Here's a summary of the discussion that followed.

A leader who believed the above might formulate a vision of where he wanted to take a team, explain it to his colleagues and seek to understand their response. This leader would reconsider his vision in the light of the responses he got and incorporate those elements that strengthened it and gave it more appeal to those who would be implementing it. The leader would then invite his colleagues to prioritise the task of planning how they would contribute to implementing the vision in their part of the team. This would be an iterative process requiring discussion, collaboration, negotiation and quite a lot of give and take with the explicit and unrelenting purpose of discovering the best course of action and one to which everybody involved could commit.

Richard said he thought that this approach to leadership would be exhausting so I wondered whether his current habit of frequently checking up on colleagues and nagging them to implement the fifty point plans he had given them was any less exhausting or any more effective in getting results. Richard admitted this was worth considering.

Richard also wondered whether his colleagues were sufficiently knowledgeable, skilled or motivated to be involved in such a process. In response, I wondered whether such a belief would limit his desire to consult with his colleagues in the first place. If he didn't consult with them how could he truly either know their current levels of knowledge, skills and motivation or hope to improve these? If on the other hand he started from the assumption that his colleagues DID have the knowledge, skills and motivation to contribute to such a process, then he would be more likely to consult with them. Richard was quiet and when he finally spoke he said he was thinking about how his current assumptions affected the choice of leadership actions he allowed himself to consider.

Richard concluded that there was value in some of the actions he had already taken. He could give me examples where some colleagues had clearly accepted his argument for the need for objective standards of behaviour in the workplace that he had expressed in public forums. These people had indeed been persuaded by objective evidence of how a reformed performance management process could transform business performance. However Richard also accepted this had not persuaded other colleagues and that there would be value in additional leadership actions. For example, he could prioritise finding the time to have an open dialogue with these colleagues about the proposed change so that they could genuinely influence and shape his thinking about the proposed change.

Richard had increased his self-awareness about his own beliefs and how they affected his actions (JUDGE becomes aware of AUTOPILOT), but could he also increase his social awareness of what was going on around him and gather new data to improve his narrative (FRIEND informs JUDGE)?

Perspective taking

In a fascinating recent study, some neuroscientists have demonstrated a link between a person's ability to take others' perspectives and their success subsequently at influencing others to act[2].

The neuroscientists observed considerably heightened activity in the *narrative neural network* (which they call 'mentalizing' network in their study) of those experimental subjects who were subsequently better able to influence others compared with their experimental subject colleagues who did not display this heightened activity. The better influencers in the experiment were taking different people's perspectives on a new idea, crucially, as they first encountered and encoded the new information rather than taking in information only from their own perspective.

This meant they…

- More accurately predicted stakeholders' interests and preferences concerning the idea
- Thought more about how to make information useful and interesting to others
- Passed on an idea to a message recipient in such a way that the message recipient wanted to recommend the idea further to others

Furthermore, the better influencers derived a sense of personal reward from this perspective taking (the brain's reward system network or 'ventral striatum' lit up).

How were the better influencers able accurately to 'mentalize' about what others thought about a new idea or take their perspective? The research didn't explore this but we might speculate that those subjects who 'mentalized' more and subsequently had more success in influencing others were also more practised at firing up their *direct experience neural network* in order to gather new data on others' perspectives. I suggest they were better able consciously to access their AUTOPILOT and ANIMAL brain processes.

What's more I speculate that they were better able to simulate the emotional state of other people (FRIEND brain processes). Their perspective taking would not just include a cognitive appreciation of another's perspective but would also include an affective appreciation too. In plain English, I speculate that the better influencers are able both to think and feel like another person by simulating the experience in their heads. Does this sound far fetched? The neuroscience provides supporting evidence that we have the brain processes to do this. Also your own intuition might convince you. Why would you cry in a movie unless you were able to simulate both another person's thinking and feeling?

Back to Richard. How could he fire up his *direct experience neural network* to gather the data he needed to understand his stakeholders' perspectives on the introduction of a new performance management process?

Exercise 2 – Social and self awareness in conversations and meetings

Richard was curious to know whether it was possible to fire up his *direct experience neural network* at will. There is evidence to suggest that people can do so and that they become better at it the more they practice[3]. I invited Richard to try the following exercise which you can also try. If you want this exercise to be really powerful then invite a third party to observe what you say and do and feedback to you what they saw and heard afterwards. This can be invaluable data for you in judging how well you use your *direct experience neural network*.

Try this:

Strike up a conversation with a colleague, friend or family member to discuss something that's really important to them.

As the conversation progresses see if you can do the following?

- Make your sole purpose for this conversation to understand their perspective or viewpoint and maintain that purpose throughout
- Focus your attention exclusively on the messages being given by them – both verbal and non-verbal
- Keep the conversation focused on what they are experiencing at this moment in time

- Do not allow thoughts of other tasks you need to do to crowd out your thinking about their experience
- Acknowledge your own responses to what they are saying and the way they say it including any feelings you may have of discomfort and awkwardness, excitement or joy
- Do this in a way that is merely reporting on your responses without judgement either on yourself or on the other person
- Vocalise your responses at appropriate moments in the conversation without interrupting their flow

Hmmm…… it can be a pretty tall order to do all that!

Debrief:

1. When the conversation is over give yourself a mark out of 10 for how well you demonstrated each of the above (1=low, 10=high). (Yes, you now have permission to judge your performance but not your self!)
2. Where you gave yourself less than 8, see if you can identify what either happened in the conversation or in your head that took you off track and write it down. Become conscious of it. For example, was there a particular word or phrase, tone of voice or action that the other person used that produced a particular emotional response in you or provoked a familiar pattern of thinking in you? Was there something you intentionally or unintentionally said or did that you noticed had produced a particular emotional response in them? If it helps write it down.
3. Remind yourself of your observations before you have the next conversation with a colleague, friend or family member to discuss something that's really important to them.

Actually, you probably do some or all of the above bulleted items in conversations a lot of the time without consciously being aware of it. I'm suggesting here that you become conscious of the times that you are firing up your *direct experience neural network*, so that you can do it in more conversations and when you choose. This should give you a sense of power or control that is pleasurable for most people.

What's the alternative? You only ever see things from your current or an historical and limited perspective. Or you are controlled by your emotional reactions to what others say and do based on what you learned from experiences in the past in situations which no longer exist. Becoming more aware of your current ways of thinking and feeling can be hugely liberating. Many people call the process 'mindfulness'.

John Teasdale, one of the leading mindfulness researchers has said, "Mindfulness is a habit, it's something the more one does, the more likely one is to be in that mode with less and less effort... it's a skill that can be learned. It's accessing something we already have. Mindfulness isn't difficult. What's difficult is to remember to be mindful."

How might this be relevant to you leading a particular change? Let's check in with Richard again. He tried the exercise above in a conversation with Patrick, one of his senior direct reports. Here's a paraphrased version of their dialogue.

Richard: "What do you think about my proposal for a new performance management process?"

Patrick: "Hmmm... it's interesting."

Richard: "OK! That sounds like you might have some reservations and that's absolutely OK."

Patrick: "The current performance management process is quite frankly seen by most of our managers as an annual box ticking exercise required by HR. In principle I think reform of the process has merit and is worth discussing as a long-term initiative but I don't see it as priority right now."

Richard: "Tell me more."

Patrick: "We're already overworked and under resourced in this directorate. We have a persistent sickness and absence problem and motivation is low in a number of areas. In addition, as you know, some key management posts that became vacant in the last few months remain unfilled. These for me are the most pressing priorities which we need to address."

As the conversation developed Richard gave Patrick the space to speak his mind. Patrick loosened up and sounded less formal, saying what he really thought and felt. At various points along the way Richard noticed in himself a number of spikes of anxiety, frustration and even anger at particular things which Patrick said, but he worked hard not to be hooked by these feelings, rather to acknowledge their presence in his head without judgement on himself or Patrick and just let them go.

Patrick continued. "I appreciate what you're trying to do with the directorate – that you're trying to get us to "up our game" especially in an environment where we have increased competition. I know this. What I would like you to appreciate is that my line reports really are very bright and capable people but once they've done the day job there just isn't time or energy for this more strategic, forward-looking work."

Richard: "Alright, I think I understand your worries and what you regard as priorities. Can I park them just for a moment – we will come back to them – so I can ask you a different question?

Patrick: "OK."

Richard: "What value, if any, do you see in the strategic, forward-looking competences I want to introduce?

Patrick: "Oh, there's potentially huge value in making the directorate think bigger picture and longer-term. I'm right with you on that. We could make much more of a difference if only we could pull our heads out of the mire of dealing with day-to-day crises."

Richard: "What would it take to allay your concerns over persistent sickness and absence and low motivation?"

Patrick: "Simple. We need to hire more people but I know that's not really an option in the current environment."

Richard: "I agree."

Patrick: "Can I speak candidly?"

Richard: "Of course."

Patrick: "There are just too many initiatives flying around here right now (Richard reported feeling a definite spike of irritation on hearing this from Patrick, acknowledged it and let it go). Can we not prioritise a few key initiatives over all others? Give people the space to focus on doing a few things very, very well? Encourage people to collaborate on those initiatives to spread the load and do them to a much higher standard?

Richard: "OK. Could we use a reformed performance management process to focus people on just those things?"

Patrick: "I don't know. How would that work?"

Richard: "I don't know exactly, but I really think it could fulfil that purpose. Does that argument make sense to you?"

Patrick: "Yes, it does."

Richard: "I wonder whether you could spend a little time thinking about how you would want to change the performance management process to focus on the things you just mentioned – prioritising a few key initiatives, giving people the space to focus on doing a few important things really well and encouraging people to collaborate to achieve higher standards?"

Patrick: "OK. That interests me."

Richard: "Now what else do you think we should be doing about sickness, absence and low morale?"

The rest of the conversation concerned the detail of key projects, initiatives and tasks which need not concern us, so let's leave the conversation between Richard and Patrick here.

After the conversation Richard reported reflecting on it – not so much from his own perspective as from Patrick's. He had noticed in the conversation for the first time an anxiety and frustration in Patrick's body language and particularly facial expressions. He had been surprised to notice Patrick's eyes briefly welling up at one point and slightly alarmed at his own feelings of upset in response. And yet, on reflection, it had given him a deeper insight into his colleague, his work circumstances and challenges. It affected Richard's thinking, feeling and subsequent leadership actions with Patrick.

What next for you?

When you next have a conversation with a colleague about a change initiative, use the seven bullet points above as your conversation guide. Here they are again:

- Make your sole purpose for this conversation to understand their perspective or viewpoint and maintain that purpose throughout
- Focus your attention exclusively on the messages being given by them – both verbal and non-verbal
- Keep the conversation focused on what they are experiencing at this moment in time
- Do not allow thoughts of other tasks you need to do to crowd out your thinking about their experience
- Acknowledge your own responses to what they are saying and the way they say it including any feelings you may have of discomfort and awkwardness, excitement or joy
- Do this in a way that is merely reporting on your responses without judgement either on yourself or on the other person
- Vocalise your responses at appropriate moments in the conversation without interrupting their flow

Then debrief on what insights that conversation has given you to:

1. Understand their enthusiasm for, or concern about, the proposed change
2. Their motivations in respect of the change (positive or negative)
3. How you might influence them

The underlying idea here is that a skilled leader is able to be truly present in a conversation with someone else. Being present with someone, listening, questioning and empathising gives the leader presence with the follower. Alvin Goldman speculates that to recognise an emotion in others, one needs to be able to experience it oneself[4]. He bases this assertion on research about people who used to be able to feel fear but who have suffered damage to the fear recognition centres in their brain, the amygdala, and who now can't experience fear and are unable to represent it to others, for example through drawing. They can depict angry, sad and disgusted faces but not fearful ones. So being present with someone relies on being able to simulate another person's thinking and feeling (JUDGE and FRIEND brain processes respectively). Why would you want to be truly present in a conversation with someone else? When you are truly present with someone else you also become influential with them and they with you. You now have the opportunity to lead or be led effectively.

Motivating with stories

Let's take stock. Effective leaders of change challenge their own and others' beliefs about what is possible and they evaluate a change idea from other people's perspectives so they can influence better. What else do they do? They tell stories.

I guess most of us can remember an example of how we were attracted to attend a presentation about something that interested us but ended up being bored to death by a flat, dull procession of Powerpoint slides from the presenter. By contrast, I guess most of us have also been to a presentation, or may be a performance of some kind, where we were riveted by what we experienced and even motivated to do something different afterwards. Effective presenters often use stories about characters who have dilemmas or opportunities with which their audience can empathise and which motivate them to act in some way[5] How does this work? Here's the neuroscience:

Our brains respond more readily to stories that distress us because they increase our production of cortisol that focuses our attention even more acutely on the source of our distress. Why? From an evolutionary perspective it makes sense to have a mechanism to focus us on the source of our distress in order to motivate us to alleviate it[6]. But compelling stories don't just distress us. They often make us feel empathy with the protagonists. They connect us with others and increase our production of oxytocin – the bonding neuro-hormone. From an evolutionary perspective it makes sense to have a hormone that facilitates bonding between a child and a parent or between adults who are codependent including codependent groups of adults. So a story which ramps up both our levels of cortisol and oxytocin is going to grab our attention, engage us with the characters and their predicament and spur us to do something to resolve both our need to reduce our distress and demonstrate empathy. Brain scans bare this out. They show the most active areas of the brain associated with responding to an emotional story are the septal area rich in oxytocin receptors (oxytocin is the bonding neuro-hormone) and those neural networks associated with creating our own narratives or stories.

I discussed this with Richard and wondered how this informed his experience of being a leader. He told me that his conscious approach to influencing others tended to revolve around presenting facts and fact-based arguments in an objective, almost detached, sort of way. But on reflection he noted that colleagues were often more motivated to change when they were able to empathise with others' perspectives.

Paul Zak reports that stories with a particular structure – the dramatic arc - are more likely to fire up our feelings of distress and empathy and motivate us to act:

Exposition	Rising action	Climax	Falling action	Denouement
The issue, challenge or situation is explained	Something grabs our attention and starts to distress us. Also we start to feel for the protagonists	The story has our full attention and we have full empathy with the protagonists	A way starts to emerge how we can act to ameliorate the situation and reduce our stress	The strands of the story all come together and a clear set of actions for us to follow presents itself

About a month after I first read this I came across a perfect example at a housing association client. Dan, the leader of the organisation's health and safety team kicked off his presentation at the start of a team building event with something close to the following words which as I listened I realised almost exactly followed the dramatic arc.

"As you know, the business wants our team to shift its role from 'doing' Health and Safety to advising line managers and enforcing standards" (Exposition)

"I don't want any of you to go through the horrible experience I went through recently on the Acacia estate in Manchester where the police and ambulance services were involved." (Rising action)

"I was there on site when a contractor fell to his death from one of our properties. If that wasn't bad enough having the police and the Health and Safety Executive crawling all over us for the next week and not knowing whether we would be prosecuted was truly horrendous." (Climax)

"As you know we weren't prosecuted but the review did reveal the need to make significant changes to our procedures and practices and their enforcement." (Falling action)

"We have the opportunity this afternoon to start planning in earnest for how we will get line managers to prioritise health and safety,

make changes to procedures and how best we can both support and police them." (Denouement)

When Dan paused briefly at the climax of his speech you could hear a pin drop in the room. He had his team's attention and more. That afternoon the team worked hard to produce a plan that would radically change the way in which they would engage with the rest of the business in order to improve health and safety. I don't know whether they would have produced that plan anyway without the team leader's speech, but when he spoke I noticed a change in the facial expressions and body language of the people in the room, even their breathing seemed to change. I concluded that the speech did make a difference to the engagement and commitment of the team to significant change. Dan had triggered some powerful FRIEND affective brain processes in his audience while providing them with the opportunity to flex their JUDGE thinking to control and channel those emotions in the afternoon session.

Exciting with a positive vision

Of course, you can also excite people with a vision of how things will be better for them and the people they care about, so long as you can empathise with them sufficiently to appreciate what will turn them on. You can even use a version of the dramatic arc to inspire people. Here's what Richard could have said to his senior management team.

"It's great for me to be able to say that this directorate has improved in leaps and bounds in recent years culminating in our very good recent government inspection. I think you can all be very proud of having a hand in those improvements." (Exposition)

"Many of us in this room have already started discussions about how we can build on those improvements so that we can differentiate what our agency offers even more clearly from rival agencies and secure our future. And if you haven't explicitly been involved in such conversations to date, I'm issuing an open invitation right now to all of you to get involved. " (Rising action)

"Imagine that in two or three years time we will be offering services and consultancy that's in a class of its own. Imagine that each of you will be involved in highly motivating and satisfying projects either in current or new areas of expertise. Imagine our reputation is improving and we're attracting increased funding from multiple, diverse sources. Imagine we're the agency that others want to emulate and learn from. Imagine we're the best at what we do." (Climax)

"Yes, I think if we are honest with ourselves and each other, we will recognise there is a gap right now between our current level of performance and where we could be. And at the same time I think we should also recognise how far we've already come." (Falling action)

"So, for me the critical question for us all concerns how can we get from where we are to where we want to be. Everyone in this room has a part to play in defining where we are going, and how we will get there. We're going to spend the rest of the day working together to start to answer those questions." (Denouement)

Exercise 3 – Creating a compelling, clear and consistent story to influence a stakeholder

1. Return to the change initiative you were considering in exercises 1 and 2. Using the dramatic arc, create a story with the express purpose of motivating a particular stakeholder to some action to implement or support the change you want.

2. How will your story create a sense of distress and empathy to engage and motivate them to act for the benefit of others? What is it that the stakeholder can do to help resolve the situation and feel a sense of relief and resolution?

OR

3. What vision of a better place in the future will your story describe that makes explicit where we are going, why we're taking the

journey, what exactly the journey will entail and precisely how we will get there.

4. Now check your narrative against the dramatic arc. Fill in any gaps and weed out any flannel. Your narrative should read like a crisp TV or web news report without digressions, repetitions and with clear, discernable progress across the arc.

Have you already made the connection with the earlier work on the *narrative neural network?* The narrative you have just created is the one you want to encourage in the minds of your stakeholders anytime they think about your change initiative. If your stakeholder doesn't adopt your narrative they may create their own different one that may lead them to behaviours you do not want.

Spreading change through networks

There's something else that effective leaders of change do. They spread their ideas through their informal networks of friends, colleagues and even (which may seem strange in the context of work-based change) through their families. These networks aren't based on hierarchy but on connection. The stronger the connection, the greater the influence of the leader. In his fascinating book 'Viral Change', Leandro Herrero[7] describes how people get things done in modern organisations. They do it more through informal unstructured relationships than through formal hierarchical reporting lines, committees or formal team meetings. So why, when we're planning how to introduce some significant piece of change to our business, department, unit or team, do we default to cascading preset messages through the hierarchy? Herrero shows how limited this approach is in achieving the change results leaders want so why would we prefer it as a way of leading change? Here again, neuroscience and human learning can shed some light on our thinking processes.

We know that the amygdala, a small, almond-shaped structure at the centre of the human brain, is central to the human experience of emotion including fear and anxiety. It is part of the ANIMAL brain processes of our model. Remember, from an evolutionary perspective it makes sense for the human brain to be sensitive to fear and anxiety first and other emotions second in order to facilitate survival of a multiplicity of threats. It also makes sense for our brains to have evolved processes that help us to learn and remember quickly (AUTOPILOT) without the need for slow, elaborate, deliberative, evaluative thinking (JUDGE). Indeed it appears that this latter form of thinking (JUDGE) is the most recent to have evolved. Emotion is central to how we learn and make meaning[8]. As our brains develop as children and teenagers, we are particularly sensitive to perceiving threats in our environment and quickly learn strategies for mitigating those threats. The amygdala helps our brains to learn fear or anxiety responses and we develop habitual, automatic, mitigating behaviours that our brains store for ready retrieval. After a while we are usually not conscious of the fear or anxiety we are feeling (ANIMAL brain processes) and the strategies we employ to alleviate them (AUTOPILOT brain processes). For example, when I feel anxious about a deadline I might not consciously be aware of it as I automatically rub my eyes or scratch my head or reach for a chocolate bar or light up a cigarette to make me feel less anxious. I probably won't even notice myself automatically opening up that same old planning template on my computer that I always use to meet a deadline whether it is truly suitable for the challenge or not.

As children we learn to conform and comply to survive and get what we want from our parents – from ice cream to attention etc. We learn to fear the social pain associated with not getting these and other things that give us a sense of reward. We also learn to adapt our behaviour to comply when parents and teachers command or coerce us to do what they want. We learn a meta lesson about how the notion of human hierarchy facilitates this – powerful and strong parents control vulnerable, weak and dependent children. So when we go to work we are already operating from automatic thinking (assumptions and mindsets) about how hierarchy facilitates how things get done in the work place. We apply our learning from home and conform and comply to survive and get what we want from our employers – from keeping our job to getting higher pay to achieving the approval of our bosses to anything else that gives us a sense of reward. We learn to fear the pain associated with not getting these rewards. So we adapt our behaviour to comply when bosses dictate or coerce us to do what they want (however subtly). We reinforce our lesson from parents about how the notion of human hierarchy facilitates all this. Powerful and strong bosses control vulnerable, weak and dependent employees! After a while, our appraisal of threat, our fear response and our resulting compliant acts become so unconscious to us that they seem like a natural order (AUTOPILOT). So when WE come to lead change it seems natural to use hierarchy, command and even coercion to make things happen.

And if it works in spreading change through an organisation, what's the problem? Well, the problem is that it doesn't work nearly as well as people think it does. Kotter and others report that most organisations only achieve about 30% of the change they want in any initiative. Herrero reports that in spite of this fact, organisations focus most of their efforts to achieve change on using the hierarchy[7]. Essentially, we've learned to default to a method of introducing change that is highly ineffective!

Why is it ineffective? What happens when you use hierarchy and coercion to achieve change? Most people comply – that means doing no more and no less than what is required of them in a contract, task, project or even job description – for fear of punishment or because, from their perspective, there is no personal motivation to do otherwise. When people comply they are not applying discretionary effort where it could make a difference, that is, the effort that is not absolutely clearly, minutely defined in the command to them delivered through the hierarchy. Here's an example from someone I coached. A manager of a call centre for an insurance company reported to me that that she had introduced a step change in customer service that required all her customer advisors to answer in coming calls within three rings. After she introduced the change, customer complaints doubled. Customers reported that advisors were indeed answering within three rings but now sounded rushed, stressed and more impolite than ever. The advisors had met the letter of the change required but many were no longer using their discretionary effort to be approachable with customers as they had done before the enforced change.

So compliance through coercive leadership often doesn't deliver the level or quality of change we want as leaders. Worse than this, coercion can produce open rebellion against the leader, the team or the organisation. Or where the rebel's fear in the presence of authority is too great for them to rebel openly, their rebellion goes underground and becomes subversion. They comply with the leader face-to-face but work frantically hard to undermine the leader behind their back. Sound familiar? It is not edifying for leader or follower and hugely corrosive of good relationships. In summary, neither compliance, rebellion nor subversion help us to affect change. What we're looking for is engagement and commitment from our followers.

So if we're not going to rely on spreading ideas and leading change through formal hierarchies how can we use our informal networks? Let's revisit Richard.

In respect of his new performance management process, who were his key stakeholders? What were his relationships like with each of them and between them?

Richard visually mapped out those people who had a significant stake either for or against the introduction of a new performance management process. Now he needed to do some analysis of the quality of the relationships on his map. Here's the exercise that he undertook which you too could also undertake in respect of the change you want to lead.

Exercise 4: Relationship quality analysis

Think of a relationship with a colleague, client or stakeholder that you want to improve. This doesn't have to be a bad relationship. It may already be an OK or good relationship but one that needs to function better to facilitate the work you are currently doing or likely to do together in the near future. It could be a relationship where you simply want to be more influential.

Either draw up your own list or use the following list of items to analyse the quality of the relationship and current level of trust. The **dear** mnemonic may help you remember these items.

1. Level of **d**isclosure
2. Level of **e**xplicitly expressed commonalities
3. Level of **a**ction that is self-less by each party for the benefit of the other
4. Level of **r**eciprocity (exchanging things/information for mutual benefit)

Give the relationship a mark out of ten against each of the above items with specific, recent examples of what's happened in the relationship that would support your marking. It's important that you can call upon evidence to support your marking.

For those items where you have scored less than 8, look at your supporting examples and ask what you would have expected to see and hear from both parties (you and them) had you been able to give a score of 8 or more.

You now have a starting list of the actions to improve this relationship. How do you get the other person to change their behaviour? Here's what I recommend. Without being aggressive or confrontational, clearly express your positive expectations of the relationship. Give the other person specific examples of the positive behaviour you want from them that you will demonstrate yourself. Then demonstrate those behaviours consistently and relentlessly!

Exercise 5: Leading change

Here's a final exercise to help you to integrate and apply what you've learned in this chapter.

1. Briefly describe a change you want to make through others.

2. What beliefs are enabling or limiting your choices of action? Where you have identified a limiting belief write down the exact opposite enabling belief. Could you believe it? What things might your enabling beliefs encourage you to do?
3. Put yourself in the shoes of one of your stakeholders. Describe what they will think and feel about your proposal
4. With the stakeholder's perspective in mind, draft a story using the dramatic arc that will move them to act. What specifically do you want the stakeholder to do / say differently?
5. Now draw a map of all the stakeholders who you need to influence to make the difference you want and prioritise which relationships you want to act on first and why.
6. Conduct a relationship quality analysis for the relationships you want to improve and act on the outcome

Notes:

1. Attending to the Present: Mindfulness Meditation Reveals Distinct Neural Modes of Self-reference, N.A.S Farb, Z.V. Segal, H. Mayberg, J. Bean, D. McKeon, Z. Fatima, and A.K. Anderson, Social Cognitive and Affective Neuroscience, 2(4),313-122, 2007
2. Creating Buzz: The Neural Correlates of Effective Message Propagation, Emily B. Falk, Sylvia A. Morelli, B. Locke Welborn, Karl Dambacher and Matthew D. Lieberman, Psychological Science, 24:1234, 2013
3. Metacognitive Awareness and Prevention of Relapse in Depression: Empirical Evidence, Teasdale J.D., Pope M., Segal Z.V., Journal of Consulting and Clinical Psychology, 70(2), 275-287, 2002
4. Simulating Minds: The Philosophy, Psychology, and Neuroscience of Mindreading, Alvin I. Goldman, 2006
5. Empathy, Neurochemistry, and the Dramatic Arc, Paul Zak at the Future of StoryTelling (video), 2012
6. An Integrative Neuroscience Platform: Application to Profiles of Negativity and Positivity Bias, E. Gordon and L. Williams, Journal of Integrative Neuroscience, Volume 7, Issue 3, September 2008. Also, Neuroception: A Subconscious System for Detecting Threats and Safety. S.W. Porges, Zero to Three: Bulletin of the National Center for Infants, Toddlers and Families, 2003
7. Viral Change, Leandro Herrero, 2006
8. The Role of Meaning and Emotion in Learning, Pat Wolfe, New Directions for Adult and Continuing Education, 110, summer 2006

3. Motivating People

Most of the leaders I have met want to motivate people to the best performance. It is central to their conception of the purpose and value of their leadership. However, many have found it difficult in practice to motivate others. Vladimir from chapter one is a good example. To be blunt, when I first met him fear and anxiety were motivating him and his team to decreasingly productive behaviour and Vladimir was only partially aware of it. During my conversations with him we explored four positive things that effective leaders do to motivate people to be more productive. They:

1. Use purpose to gain commitment
2. Encourage autonomy to gain innovation
3. Encourage mastery to gain high quality
4. Facilitate connection to gain discretionary effort (or going the extra mile)

'It is better to be feared than loved'[1] Really?

Before we explore each of the four positive motivators listed above, we need to explore the motivator of fear. It is often the first emotion on the scene when people interact with each other in the work place, so let's deal with it first. Effective leaders know that fear destroys all of the above positive motivators and their associated business benefits. In contrast, every tyrant and bully in history has learned that fear is a powerful human motivator to compliance and passivity. Compliance is not commitment. Compliance and passivity do not produce innovation, high quality or discretionary effort. If we are to avoid being both compliant and passive and provoking compliance and passivity in others, it helps to understand how fear and motivation work in the human brain.

Neuroscientists and psychologists are still discovering exactly how our brains operate when we experience fear. However, there is already a considerable amount of agreement about the nature of the brain processes they have observed so far. Sometimes our fear is an automatic and often unconscious response to perceived threats in the external environment (see ANIMAL in diagram below). At other times our fear is provoked by our own internal, learned patterns of thinking (AUTOPILOT).

Brain Processes	Cognitive (Thinking) Purpose: True or false	Affective (Feeling) Purpose: Avoid or approach
Controlled • serial • effortful • evoked deliberately • good introspective access	J U D G E	F R I E N D
Automatic • parallel • effortless • reflexive • poor introspective access	A U T O P I L O T	A N I M A L

Kevin Ochsner and James Gross[2] report that events outside us can trigger fear in us that motivates us to action. This involves automatic brain processes detecting danger outside our conscious awareness and motivating us to act fast. We only become consciously aware of the feeling of fear after we have acted. An example would be when somebody unexpectedly shouts "Boo!' in our face and we involuntarily jump or raise our hand in protection. Only afterwards, when top-level brain processes have kicked in, we consciously evaluate the situation and realise that somebody was simply playing a game with us. Our top-level brain processes then send signals to dampen down the brain processes producing the sensation of fear, switching off the motivation for further action.

If you believe that fear never motivates you to say or do things at work, let me ask you this. Have you ever walked in to a meeting and before you even sat down were vaguely aware of feeling uncomfortable but couldn't put your finger on it? It's not a sixth sense! Your five, real senses (which have clearly identifiable brain processes) have provided some data that has automatically triggered a threat response in you. You may well be unconscious of the precise nature of the data. The discomfort is your motivator to do something to survive the perceived threat. Most of the things you might be motivated to do or say will fall into one or of the following categories (which may be familiar to you), namely - flight, fight or freeze.

Ochsner and Gross also report that our own patterns of thinking can provoke fear in us that motivates us to action. During one of our coaching sessions, Vladimir provided me with an excellent example. It became clear during our conversation that Vladimir had learned from colleagues that the bank considered employees who didn't achieve promotion within two years of appointment as failures. In spite of being an experienced banker with a good track record of successful deals over two years, Vladimir had still not achieved a promotion on the second anniversary of his appointment. His discussions with his line manager revealed no clear promotional opportunities for him any time soon. (The bank was actively pursuing a flatter structure to strip out cost in a recessionary economic climate.) However, Vladimir started ruminating that the bank was beginning to view him as a failure and this provoked an increasing sense of fear in him that he was going to be sidelined or even sacked. This feeling grew every time he suspected that he was being evaluated for his competence and commitment by senior colleagues. He suspected this even though nobody ever explicitly said that they were evaluating him or provided any judgement about him. Vladimir was effectively undermining his own confidence.

Vladimir's fear increasingly motivated him to act in more compliant and passive ways with both senior colleagues and external partners, doing no more or less than was explicitly required of him. His colleagues now started to notice him demonstrating a little less commitment and innovation in his work, a small drop in quality in some areas and noticeably less discretionary effort over all. Ironically, some colleagues now openly inferred from this evidence that Vladimir was less motivated than when he started in post and probably not yet ready for promotion whenever that became a possibility.

The impact of Vladimir's fear did not end with Vladimir. In his desire to be more compliant and passive with both senior colleagues and external partners, he started to allow a lot less freedom to his subordinate colleagues in how they went about their work, in spite of their high levels of experience. His overriding concern became the need to limit any criticism, however small, of his subordinate colleagues' work from people either in or outside his department so that the bank had no grounds for sacking him. He became expert at imagining scenarios in which the work of his colleagues might go wrong or be criticised. At best these scenarios were unlikely with little real impact on the perceived positive value of what his colleagues produced and at worst fanciful, based on flimsy intuition and unsupported by hard evidence. However, Vladimir's subordinate colleagues gradually accepted this limitation on their freedom of working and became ever more anxious themselves about what might go wrong in their jobs. It became the norm for how the department functioned, from how meetings were conducted to the structure, content and tone of colleagues' reports to internal or external customers. The atmosphere of anxiety became tangible when some of Vladimir's colleagues were required to make a presentation of the department's work to colleagues from other departments. Vladimir's instinct was to make the presentation himself but he was away on business during the only time available for preparation. He instructed his subordinate colleagues to prepare a presentation and insisted on previewing it two hours before the actual event. During that preview, Vladimir fired a series of unlikely and unsubstantiated objections and interruptions at his subordinate colleagues, effectively undermining their confidence and motivation for the presentation ahead. With little time remaining Vladimir and his colleagues cobbled together a new, disjointed presentation which lost the flow of the original and which he and his colleagues delivered looking and sounding uncertain and frankly fearful in front of their colleagues from other departments. It was received with bemusement by some and disappointment by most.

What could Vladimir learn from neuroscience that might shed light on his predicament? Three pieces of information came to mind:

1. We tend to perceive threats and deal with them before opportunities[3]. However, we also have the thinking capacity (JUDGE brain processes) to work out how fear is triggering us to inappropriate and negative actions
2. We learn patterns of thinking which can produce fear in us but we have the capacity to overwrite those patterns[4]
3. Our own behaviour as leaders can either create fear in others or positive emotions

Exercise 1: Removing fear as a motivator

Here's an exercise which I invited Vladimir to do and which you could do too. The purpose of the exercise is to become consciously aware of why, what and how fear motivates you at work, who contributes and when and where it happens. If you know these things you can stop fear motivating you to inappropriate actions that you later regret. As you work through the questions you may find yourself questioning your current mindset and replacing it with a more positive, open one.

1. What has fear motivated you to do at work recently? If you don't like the word 'fear' substitute the word 'anxiety'. Don't get caught up in re-experiencing the feeling of fear. Simply report on its impact on your actions.
2. How did you rationalise your actions? What assumptions about the situation were you working from? What evidence if any supported your rationalisation? Where was the evidence lacking or flimsy? What evidence might have contradicted your rationalisation?
3. What specifically provoked the feeling of fear or anxiety, i.e. somebody's actions or words or a familiar pattern of your own thoughts?

4. What narrative or story did you create to make sense of the situation? What's a different, more positive narrative? Could you believe it? What actions would the more positive narrative enable you to pursue in this situation?

Practising this type of analysis on a regular and frequent basis can help you to remove fear as a motivator by deconstructing the narrative you have invented. Then you can focus on substituting the following positive motivators in your working life.

Using purpose to gain commitment

People are motivated by knowledge about why they are doing something and the difference it makes[5]. We could examine this at two levels, macro and micro. At the macro level, people find it motivating to know what the big picture cause is to which the organisation is committed or its mission, and why that will make the world a better place. At the micro level, people find it motivating to know what precisely they themselves do at work that adds the most value, who values it and why. People also find it motivating to know explicitly how their individual, micro purpose contributes to the organisational, macro purpose.

Exercise 2 – Using purpose to gain commitment

1. What is it about your organisation's mission or purpose that excites you?
2. When your organisation is achieving its mission or purpose what will you notice people both outside and inside the organisation doing differently?
3. What three projects/tasks in your current role add the most value? Who values them and why? How much of your effort is currently focused on these priorities?
4. What one project/task would add as least as much if not more value than the three you have already identified?
5. How precisely do these high value added projects/tasks contribute toward the organisation's mission? What's your evidence? How could you make them contribute more? How

could they help to make the organisation's mission more tangible?

You could now use these questions to start a conversation with a colleague to discuss how to maximise their motivation.

Using autonomy to gain innovation

People love having power and autonomy at work[6]. However, giving people power to meet their own challenges and innovate solutions does not mean abandoning them to do it all alone. An effective leader coaches a colleague to apply effort, creativity and tenacity to problem solving. An effective leader can coach a colleague to become aware of their current patterns of thinking (AUTOPILOT) and challenge limiting beliefs, mindsets and assumptions. They can also coach a colleague to become aware of when they have been triggered into a negative emotion (ANIMAL) and help them to accept the emotion without judgement on themselves or others and let go of it (JUDGE). They can help a colleague to reappraise a situation, conversation or relationship in a more positive way (JUDGE). They can invite them to see a situation or conversation from another's perspective (firing up FRIEND to inform JUDGE). They can help the colleague to decide a new goal for whatever is challenging them and plot a new course forward (JUDGE over rides AUTOPILOT and ANIMAL). They can help them to discriminate between situations when it is OK to rely on automatic patterns of thinking, and situations where new thinking is required. They can help them to notice more in their interactions with colleagues and improve the quality of their thinking (i.e. help the coachee to fire up their *direct experience neural network* to inform their *narrative neural network* better. (See 'Challenging Beliefs' section in chapter 2.)

For better or worse

Viewed through the lens of our brain processes model, here's how our thinking in a new coaching situation could make us act more effectively.

71

Brain Processes	Cognitive (Thinking) Purpose: True or false	Affective (Feeling) Purpose: Avoid or approach
Controlled • serial • effortful • evoked deliberately • good introspective access	J U D G E e.g. Ask questions to help coachee become aware of emotional triggers, assumptions and to empathise better Feed back and test observations of coachees' behaviour and what you have inferred from them Invite coachee to share their observations of their own and other people's behaviour and what they have inferred from them Challenge coachee to substantiate their inferences with evidence	F R I E N D e.g. Empathise with coachee to understand their situation and perspective better Use that understanding to inform coaching questions, feedback, observations and challenges
Automatic • parallel • effortless • reflexive • poor introspective access	A U T O P I L O T e.g. Use tried and tested coaching assumptions and mindsets where they are still proven and relevant	A N I M A L e.g. Check out impressions and intuitions about the coachee to see how real they are

In contrast, here's how our thinking in a new coaching situation could make us act ineffectively.

Think worse, coach worse

Brain Processes	Cognitive (Thinking) Purpose: True or false	Affective (Feeling) Purpose: Avoid or approach
Controlled • serial • effortful • evoked deliberately • good introspective access	JUDGE e.g. I start to solve the coachee's problem for them in my own mind and stop listening and questioning	FRIEND e.g. I over empathise with the coachee and lose my objectivity
Automatic • parallel • effortless • reflexive • poor introspective access	AUTOPILOT e.g. I assume that if a coachee looks and sounds like they don't understand a problem then they don't have the capacity to work it out	ANIMAL e.g. The chemistry with the coachee just doesn't feel right so I abandon my attempts at coaching

Exercise 3 - Using autonomy to gain innovation

You can use this exercise to practice coaching a colleague so that they take responsibility for a particular challenge and produce their own innovative solution. Apart from the first bullet, this is more of a menu of possible coaching actions you can employ than a strict sequence.

- Ask the coachee to outline their challenge to you
- Ask them about the:
    a) Assumptions they are working from
    b) Thinking processes they are using
    c) Sources of evidence they are choosing from and why
    d) Emotions that have triggered them to action so far
    e) Perspectives of other people who have a stake in their challenge
- Feedback and test with them what you have observed of their behaviour and what you have inferred from it
- Invite them to share what they have observed of their own and other people's behaviour and what they have inferred from them
- Challenge them to substantiate their inferences with evidence and invite them to question their own inferences with counter evidence
- Invite them to identify and challenge any assumptions which are limiting their choice of actions
- Explore more enabling assumptions with them and the actions which might flow from these
- Invite them to plan a new course of action to which they will commit
- Both enjoy a well-earned coffee/tea!

You'll notice that with this type of coaching you always keep the responsibility for meeting the challenge with your coachee. You are challenging their thinking not their power or autonomy.

Using mastery to gain high quality

People love being really good at something[7]. However, there is no guarantee that that something will be even remotely work related. The challenge for you and me as leaders is to develop people to be really good at things that will contribute directly to raising quality at work. It is even better if we can link a colleague's pursuit of quality to major business improvements in areas such as better customer service, better products and services, smarter use of technology, more efficient processes, better employee behaviour, encouraging and inspiring the best from others etc. Effective leaders channel their colleagues' desire for mastery towards whatever the organisation needs to improve.

Exercise 4 - Using mastery to gain high quality

- Meet with a colleague and explain that you want to find out what they think they're really good at. Say that you want to know as much about what they're good at outside as inside work. Make sure that your assessment is based on objective evidence, not just on their (or your) opinion. Dig a bit to find out specifically what knowledge or skills they are using that motivate them, for example, mathematical, spatial, language, analytical, big picture, detail, people-related, kinaesthetic, artistic, musical etc. What is it about the thing they're good at that gives them satisfaction or excitement? The more specific they can be the better. The more conscious they become of it in conversation with you the better. I'm guessing that you've rarely or never asked questions that probe this deeply into most of your colleagues' motivations

- Now ask them something like "In an ideal world where you had total control over your priorities and time at work, on what projects would you focus your efforts and why?"

- Using the information you have gathered, start matching what they're good at with projects to improve the business

- Discuss your thoughts with the colleague and initiate a discussion about why and how they might start to prioritise the projects to improve the business

Using connection to gain discretionary effort (or going the extra mile)

People love to belong to a group, troop, family, tribe etc.[8] We are wired to work hard for groups with which we identify. We are concerned about status because it signifies that others value us and that we have a place of importance in the group and therefore are connected to the group. We are concerned about fairness so that we can be certain that the group will meet both our needs and the needs of other group members so that we stay connected and supportive. When we feel connected we use the same neural circuitry to experience social pleasure as we use to feel physical pleasure. When we feel excluded or isolated we use the same neural circuitry to experience social pain as we use to feel physical pain. The neural architecture is there to make us exert ourselves for the group.

Exercise 5 - Using connection to gain discretionary effort (or going the extra mile)

- What groups at work do you belong and feel connected to (a group can be as small as you and one other person)?
- Describe a couple of recent occasions when your sense of belonging and connection to a group motivated you to discretionary effort or 'going the extra mile'. How did 'going the extra mile' make you feel?
- What groups do you need to feel connected to in order to do your job better? Note this is not the same question as 'What groups do you currently *want* to feel connected to?' Your answer to the 'need' question should factor in what the business needs from you. Your answer to the '*want*' question is likely to be based on your personal likes and dislikes of individual personalities. As an effective leader you need to answer the former question.
- What things could you do to demonstrate discretionary effort or 'going the extra mile' with the groups to which you need to feel connected?
- What are you going to do to take this forward?

You could use these questions in a discussion with a colleague about maximising their motivation.

What happened when Vladimir did the exercises?

Exercise 1: Removing fear as a motivator

1. What has fear motivated you to do at work recently? If you don't like the word 'fear' substitute the word 'anxiety'. Don't get caught up in re-experiencing the feeling of fear. Simply report on its impact on your actions.
2. How did you rationalise your actions? What assumptions about the situation were you working from? What evidence if any supported your rationalisation? Where was the evidence lacking or flimsy? What evidence might have contradicted your rationalisation?
3. What specifically provoked the feeling of fear or anxiety, i.e. somebody's actions or words or a familiar pattern of your own thoughts?
4. What narrative or story did you create to make sense of the situation? What's a different, more positive narrative? Could you believe it? What actions would the more positive narrative enable you to pursue in this situation?

Vladimir:

1. *I have chosen to seek investment for small, safe projects for which we can pretty much guarantee funding with little or no effort. I fear for my reputation, job and particularly fear losing my boss' support should I choose to pursue more risky projects in areas which, admittedly, would deliver considerably more towards the bank's stated, big picture objectives and strategy.*
2. *We need a climate of much greater economic and political certainty before we embark on these more risky projects. If I worked to get these projects funded and failed to do so I would take all the blame and look bad.*
3. *My boss reacted very negatively when I first recommended including a few higher risk projects in my portfolio.*
4. *My boss has had his fingers burned in the past and thinks his reputation is damaged. He thinks that if I fail this would reflect badly on him and worsen his reputation still further. The opposite narrative is that the bank will support us both if*

we take limited, clearly defined risks and we are utterly transparent in what we doing, why, how and the outcomes including lessons learned for the future. If we believed this we could consider how we might put significant effort into researching and really understanding just how risky the higher risk projects actually are rather than indulging in much guess work as we currently are doing.

Exercise 2 – Using purpose to gain commitment

1. What is it about your organisation's mission or purpose that excites you?
2. When your organisation is achieving its mission or purpose what will you notice people both outside and inside the organisation doing differently?
3. What three projects/tasks in your current role add the most value? Who values them and why? How much of your effort is currently focused on these priorities?
4. What one project/task would add as least as much if not more value than the three you have already identified?
5. How precisely do these high value added projects/tasks contribute toward the organisation's mission? What's your evidence? How could you make them contribute more? How could they help to make the organisation's mission more tangible?

Vladimir:

1. *Part of the bank's mission is to explore new forms of investment suitable for emergent world markets. I am particularly interested in projects to help SMEs in such markets access investment where the political, economic, social or cultural environment currently creates barriers. My wife's family has a history of setting up and growing successful businesses so I have a personal commitment to this sector.*
2. *Outside our organisation, we will see many more SMEs seeking out and accessing local investment resources. We will have evidence that they know who to contact in their*

local business communities to access investment and how to make their case effectively for that investment. Inside our organisation, we will have leaders and project teams executing well-researched plans to making this happen.

3. The three projects where I can add the most value in my role are (1) building a broader and deeper network of banking, legal, environmental experts internally at the bank who I can draw in to project teams (2) reviewing our processes for sourcing people for project teams (3) working with others to reform our processes for deal submission and evaluation. I currently spend about 10% of my time on these projects.

4. I don't want one more project of equal value to the above. I do want to spend nearer 50% of my time on the above three projects. Improvements in these three areas would save me from much current firefighting and save me significant amounts of time and effort currently spent on low value-added activity.

5. Building a broader and deeper network of banking, legal, environmental (etc.) experts internally who I can draw in to project teams means we are better able to set up more, better quality and more sustainable investment opportunities for SMEs. Reviewing our processes for sourcing people for project teams means we will get higher quality input to our projects. Working with others to reform our processes for deal submission and evaluation is an opportunity to become far more sensitive to the political, economic, social or cultural environments in which we operate and therefore more likely to succeed with our offering.

Exercise 3 - Using autonomy to gain innovation

- Ask the coachee to outline their challenge to you
- Ask them about the:
  a) Assumptions they are working from
  b) Thinking processes they are using
  c) Sources of evidence they are choosing from and why
  d) Emotions that have triggered them to action so far
  e) Perspectives of other people who have a stake in their challenge

- Feedback and test with them what you have observed of their behaviour and what you have inferred from it
- Invite them to share what they have observed of their own and other people's behaviour and what they have inferred from them
- Challenge them to substantiate their inferences with evidence and invite them to question their own inferences with counter evidence
- Invite them to identify and challenge any assumptions which are limiting their choice of actions
- Explore more enabling assumptions with them and the actions which might flow from these
- Invite them to plan a new course of action to which they will commit
- Both enjoy a well-earned coffee/tea!

Vladimir:

Here is rough transcript of the coaching conversation that I had with my colleague Bashir.

Vladimir: "Bashir. You said a couple of months ago that you wanted to be considered for promotion so I got you involved with the Egypt project and introduced you to Hassan and Steve. Your latest report suggests that you're not making much progress. What's the problem?"

Bashir: "Well, I have to say Vladimir that this is a very difficult project you have given me. As you know I met with Hassan and Steve who put me in contact with the Cairo team and this is where all the problems come from."

Vladimir: "What do you mean?"

Bashir: "The Cairo team just don't listen to me. I tell them what to do and they don't do it. They keep coming up with more and more obstacles, barriers and problems. I say to them that it is their job to remove those obstacles. It's why the bank is using their expertise in the first place. But they just don't get it."

Vladimir: "What exactly don't they get and why?"

Bashir: "Look, they have their own targets to meet and they have had to make staff cuts this year and nobody wants to take on more work with fewer people, especially if there is no link to a bonus."

Vladimir: "They told you this?"

Bashir: "Well, not in so many words, but why wouldn't they think that way? We think that way here."

Vladimir: "So that's how you think?"

Bashir: "Yes, for sure. Who doesn't?"

Vladimir: "Well, I wonder if we can assume the Cairo team really does think that way without explicit evidence. Is it possible they think a different way?"

Bashir: "It's possible."

Vladimir: "You said they keep coming up with more and more obstacles, barriers and problems with your instructions to them."

Bashir: "Yes."

Vladimir: "And that they are doing this because they have their own targets to meet?"

Bashir: "Yes."

Vladimir: "So have you linked those two things together?"

Bashir: "Yes. It's a logical link."

Vladimir: "OK. What evidence supports you making that link?"

Bashir: "Hmmm……well, I don't have any specific evidence."

Vladimir: "Are you prepared to consider some alternative reasons why the Cairo team keeps coming up with obstacles, barriers and problems with your instructions to them?"

Bashir: "OK."

Vladimir: "So what other reasons could there be?"

Bashir: "Oh, I don't know….. may be they're just lazy!"

Vladimir: "I don't think so! Their figures for the last quarter show them as one of the highest performing teams. Might there be some reasons associated with the fact that you instructed them, or the way in which you instructed them?"

Bashir: "OK, so I think you're saying may be they don't like me instructing them what to do. The way I see it, I am the project leader so they're expecting me to have a clear plan for how they will achieve the project objectives."

Vladimir: "How do you know they expect you to have a plan?"

Bashir: "Well, I've assumed that."

Vladimir: "Is it possible your assumption is wrong?"

Bashir: "Yes, it is possible."

Vladimir: "What if you assumed they did NOT expect you to have a plan? How would you deal with the situation differently then."

Bashir: "If I believed they were not expecting a plan from me, I would set the objectives and ask them to provide me with their own ideas for a plan. But if I did that I would not be leading the project would I?"

Vladimir: "Why not?"

Bashir: "The Cairo team would have considerable control over the project and I would have less control."

Vladimir: "What good might come of the Cairo team having more control?"

Bashir: "What good might come of them having more control? Hmmm....may be they might be more committed to the project. They might bring their expertise to bear more readily. But there would be a risk to me and my reputation."

Vladimir: "How much do you know about their expertise and commitment?"

Bashir: "Hmmm.....I don't really know that much about what they're good at......I need to go and find out more."

Vladimir: "How will you do that?"

Bashir: "I need to set up a number of conference calls and probably a visit very soon to find out. I need to think carefully what questions I need answers to."

Exercise 4 - Using mastery to gain high quality

- Meet with a colleague and explain that you want to find out what they think they're really good at. Say that you want to know as much about what they're good at outside as inside work. Make sure that your assessment is based on objective evidence, not just on their (or your) opinion. Dig a bit to find out specifically what knowledge or skills they are using that motivate them, for example, mathematical, spatial, language, analytical, big picture, detail, people-related, kinaesthetic, artistic, musical etc. What is it about the thing they're good at that gives them satisfaction or excitement? The more specific they can be the better. The more conscious they become of it in conversation with you the better. I'm guessing that you've rarely or never asked questions that probe this deeply into most of your colleagues' motivations

- Now ask them something like "In an ideal world where you had total control over your priorities and time at work, on what projects would you focus your efforts and why?"

- Using the information you have gathered, start matching what they're good at with projects to improve the business

- Discuss your thoughts with the colleague and initiate a discussion about why and how they might start to prioritise the projects to improve the business

Vladimir:

Here's another rough transcript of the conversation I had with Bashir two weeks on from the last one.

Vladimir: "Hi Bashir. I can't believe it's already been a couple of weeks since we last spoke. How are you?"

Bashir: "I'm good, thank you, and you?"

Vladimir: "I'm good too, thank you. I heard your trip to meet the Cairo team went well. They were really appreciative of you taking the time to explain the project objectives and why the bank is supporting this initiative. How do you think the meeting went?"

Bashir: "It went well. I was pleasantly surprised how interested and motivated they were when we got talking about the purpose of the project and how much the bank wants it. When we started talking about planning and implementation, they were almost competing amongst themselves to create ideas."

Vladimir: "Well that's great!......You know we haven't ever really talked about what projects really excite you personally and I'd really like to know a bit more about what motivates you so I can get you involved in suitable projects, if you're interested. I also want to find out what you think you're really good at both outside as well as inside work. So first off, what projects have really interested you recently and why?"

Bashir: "Hmmm.....I think I need to think about this a bit before answering......"

Vladimir: "Fine, take your time."

Bashir: "...........well, I guess the bank appointed me for my technical skills and, don't get me wrong, I enjoy the technical side of my work. But I've been doing mostly technical for about five years now and I really would like to get more involved in policy making – you know the bigger picture. I think I have a good understanding of how the bank currently works and I think I could contribute significantly to improving policy development. I had a policy creation brief in my last role before coming to this bank. I've also contributed quite a lot of time and effort to the policy review team here following the Armenia pharma and the Serbian gas deals."

Vladimir: "Oh really! I didn't know that."

Bashir: "Yes, I was talking to Olga and Serpil in the policy review team. I guess I was keen for them to know some of things we had learned in recent times and how that might contribute to policy development."

Vladimir: "Yes and what things did you learn?"

Bashir: "Well the main thing was that we had assumed a much more sophisticated understanding of international banking practice than was readily available amongst many of the clients on those projects. I was able to give Olga and Serpil some detailed examples which really made them sit up and pay attention."

Vladimir: "So policy development interests you. What skills do you bring to it?"

Bashir: *"I guess I just have a natural tendency to want to apply what we learn at the highest level. It often seems to me that when we debrief what worked and didn't work on projects we miss drawing conclusions for how the organisation as a whole could work better and fulfill its mission more effectively. Most people don't get beyond drawing up a list of obvious pitfalls in their own immediate area to be avoided next time round. And they rarely share their insights with their colleagues. It's not because they are selfish or lazy. It's just not part of their mindset to do that. It is part of my mindset to do it. Carrying those sorts of reviews and feeding them into the bank's policy creation process really interests me at this stage in my career."*

Vladimir: *"Look, why don't you and I meet with Matteo, Head of Policy to explore ways in which you might take this forward for everyone's benefit. I'll be completely transparent with you Bashir, I have my own interest here. I am committed to working with others in this bank to reform our processes for deal submission and evaluation. Working with the policy team is going to be central to that so I'm keen to forge links between us and them and you could help me to do that. What do you think?"*

Bashir: *"Sounds good!"*

Exercise 5 - Using connection to gain discretionary effort (or going the extra mile)

- What groups at work do you belong and feel connected to (a group can be as small as you and one other person)?
- Describe a couple of recent occasions when your sense of belonging and connection to a group motivated you to discretionary effort or 'going the extra mile'. How did 'going the extra mile' make you feel?
- What groups do you need to feel connected to in order to do your job better? Note this is not the same question as 'What groups do you currently *want* to feel connected to?' Your answer to the 'need' question should factor in what the business needs from you. Your answer to the '*want*' question

is likely to be based on your personal likes and dislikes of individual personalities. As an effective leader you need to answer the former question.

- What things could you do to demonstrate discretionary effort or 'going the extra mile' with the groups to which you need to feel connected?
- What are you going to do to take this forward?

Vladimir

Bashir and I continued our conversation and I asked him with which groups of people he felt particularly connected at the bank.

Bashir: "Like I said, I've spent quite a lot of time with the policy review team in recent months and I really admire the work they do. In particular, I'm interested in their work on the bank's policies on environmental ethics."

Vladimir: "Well I know working with policy review has been part of your remit for this year but I didn't realise it had become so important to you. How has it impacted you role?"

Bashir: "It's become a bit of passion of mine! I really think it's brought out the best in me. I enjoy reviewing big projects, making the connections with project implementers and building the relationships and trust to a level where these people are open and honest with me about the real lessons to be learned. It isn't easy work a lot of the time because some people in the bank can be initially protective about sharing information. But I have been truly motivated to work with them and put in the hours and the effort."

Vladimir: "Looking forward, with which groups do you still need to connect in order to do your job better?"

Bashir: "There are people like Henri in (department X) and Patricia in (department Y) who I don't really know but whose experience I keep hearing could really help to improve my input to policy development. These and others are the people I need to talk to."

Vladimir: "So what next to take this forward?"

Bashir: "OK, so here are the specifics of what I'd like to do....."

Notes:

1. The Prince, Niccolo Machiavelli, 1532
2. The Neural Architecture of Emotion Regulation, Kevin N. Ochsner and James J. Gross, Handbook of Emotion Regulation, edited by James J. Gross, 2007
3. An Integrative Neuroscience Platform: Application to Profiles of Negativity and Positivity Bias, E. Gordon and L. Williams, Journal of Integrative Neuroscience, Volume 7, Issue 3, September 2008. Also, Neuroception: A Subconscious System for Detecting Threats and Safety. S.W. Porges, Zero to Three: Bulletin of the National Center for Infants, Toddlers and Families, 2003
4. Neural Mechanisms of Extinction Learning and Retrieval, Gregory J Quirk and Devin Mueller, Neuropsychopharmacology, 33, 56–72, 2008. Also, The Neural Bases of Attitudes, Emily B.C. Falk, Matthew D. Lieberman, from The Neural Basis of Human Belief Systems, 71-94, 2013. Also, Cognitive Neuroscience of Emotional Memory, Kevin S LaBar and Roberto Cabeza, Nature Reviews Neuroscience 7, 54-64, 2006. Also, The Emotional Brain: The Mysterious Underpinnings of Emotional Life, Joseph E.LeDoux, 1998.
5. Drive: The Surprising Truth About What Motivates Us, Daniel H. Pink, 2009
6. Drive: The Surprising Truth About What Motivates Us, Daniel H. Pink, 2009
7. Drive: The Surprising Truth About What Motivates Us, Daniel H. Pink, 2009
8. Social: Why We are Wired to Connect, Matthew D. Liebermann, 2013

4. Dealing with 'difficult' personalities

"You know Jonathan, my job would be so much easier if I didn't have such 'difficult' personalities in the senior management team."

This is what Stella told me in her first coaching session. You may remember from Chapter 1 that Stella is a confident and capable senior manager in a media company. However, she struggles to get her points across to senior management colleagues whom she regards variously as arrogant, intimidating and unrealistic. In case you were wondering, she suffers both women and men with 'difficult' personalities.

I would like to assert that it is not other people's personalities per se which we find difficult but handling our own emotional reactions to specific things which people say and do. The neuroscientist Joseph LeDoux[1] wrote, "While conscious control over emotions is weak, emotions can flood consciousness. This is so because the wiring of the brain at this point in our evolutionary history is such that connections from the emotional systems to the cognitive systems are stronger than connections from the cognitive systems to the emotional systems." So are we inevitably slaves to our emotions? I think the answer is 'No, but it requires effort not to be'. I also think that we have the potential to learn how to recognise our emotions, accept them and, if we want to, move on from them. We can learn to recognise situations and interactions that trigger us into unwanted emotions and learn ways of dealing with them. When we first do this it can feel like a huge effort but if we persist and practice we can make it effortless. There is a similarity here with learning to drive a car. When you had your first driving lesson there was an almost overwhelming amount of information to pay attention to and deal with. It felt effortful. When you became an experienced driver you automatically noticed potential dangers and acted appropriately and effectively and then it felt effortless. Similarly, when you first deal with a 'difficult' new behaviour from another person it can feel effortful. When you gain experience you automatically notice your emotional reactions to 'difficult' people and act appropriately and effectively and it starts to feel effortless.

Roy Baumeister[2] has demonstrated that both self-control (including controlling our emotions) and cognitive effort are forms of mental work drawing at least partly on a shared pool of mental energy. His research found that an effort of will or self control is tiring; if you have had to force yourself to do something, you are less willing or less able to exert self control when the next challenge comes around. What's more we also know that exerting self-control is significantly more difficult when we consume alcohol, have insufficient sleep or not enough glucose. But there's also good news! Our brains have the capacity to convert effortful, evaluative, energy-sapping, controlled thinking in to effortless, reflexive, energy-saving, automatic thinking. In terms of our brain processes model (see diagram below), this is the capacity to move a task from JUDGE to AUTOPILOT. The trick is to recognise when it's OK to rely on the energy-saving, automatic thinking and when the situation demands effortful, controlled thinking. How do we improve our ability to recognise which situation pertains? We can improve our ability to gather data with which to perceive a situation and make a judgement. For example, we can improve our conscious awareness of other people's facial expressions, words and tone of voice and body language, the interactions between people, and our own emotional responses. In chapter 2 we talked about firing up some brain processes called our *direct experience neural network* which we'll explore some more in the context of this chapter. (See 'Challenging Beliefs' section in chapter 2.)

In our coaching conversations I shared with Stella what I have learned about how effective leaders deal with 'difficult' personalities. Effective leaders:

1. Recognise that the true difficulty lies not in the personality of the other person but in their own current thinking, feeling and actions and that they can change these
2. Seek to become more consciously aware of how they are appraising a conversation or situation in terms of threat or reward and the narrative they are creating
3. Identify and regulate their emotions
4. Virtually simulate others' experiences in their minds to empathise better

5. Actively build relationships by seeking common ground first and exploring differences second

What insights to Stella's own situation might the above offer? We'll examine the above items and then see what sense they helped Stella to make of her situation.

Understanding your thinking, feeling and actions

Let's briefly revisit our model of brain processes from chapter 1 and focus in particular on ANIMAL and AUTOPILOT.

Brain Processes	Cognitive (Thinking) Purpose: True or false	Affective (Feeling) Purpose: Avoid or approach
Controlled • serial • effortful • evoked deliberately • good introspective access	J U D G E	F R I E N D
Automatic • parallel • effortless • reflexive • poor introspective access	A U T O P I L O T	A N I M A L

Feelings and impressions first

Let's focus on ANIMAL brain processes first. Why? Because they are the first on the scene when you appraise a new situation. ANIMAL brain processes are designed to appraise very quickly whether this new situation is either a threat or an opportunity and motivate you to act accordingly. Do you remember our example from the last chapter? Here it is again:

Have you ever walked in to a meeting and before you even sat down were vaguely aware of feeling uncomfortable but couldn't put your finger on it? It's not a sixth sense! Your five, real senses (which have clearly identifiable brain processes) have provided some data that has automatically triggered a threat response in you. You may well be unconscious of the data. The discomfort is your motivator to do something to survive the perceived threat. Most of the things you might be motivated to do or say will fall into one or of the following categories (which may be familiar to you), namely - flight, fight or freeze.

Here's the flip example. Have you ever walked in to a meeting and before you even sat down were vaguely aware of feeling comfortable but couldn't put your finger on it? It's still not a sixth sense! Your five, real senses have provided some data that has automatically triggered an opportunity seeking response in you. The comfort is your motivator to explore, uncover and seize the perceived opportunity.

ANIMAL brain processes work very fast (compared with processes in other parts of our model) and achieve their speed because they deal in impressions, intuitions, intentions and feelings rather than cold, hard, fact-driven logic. But the speed of response is sometimes achieved at the cost of inaccuracy of appraisal of the new situation. We can be triggered into impressions and feelings that motivate us to inappropriate actions. For example:

- The boss grimaces at you for a microsecond which makes you feel threatened. This does not mean it is appropriate to agree unthinkingly to the demand she now makes

- Your direct report's body language matches the distress of a child. This does not mean that it is appropriate to come to his rescue
- Your colleague uses a tone of voice that matches the disapproval of a parent. This does not mean it is appropriate to feel chastised
- "I felt he was trustworthy so I unquestioningly accepted his business plan."

Exercise 1 – Triggered feelings

Here's a quick exercise that I invited Stella to do that you could do too. Briefly describe a recent occasion when you were triggered into a feeling that motivated you to an action which, with hindsight, was inappropriate or that you later regretted. You can build on this exercise as we work through the chapter so when you've made your description just park it for now.

Automatic thinking

Now let's focus on AUTOPILOT brain processes. In any situation in which we find ourselves our brain seeks patterns of similarity to previous situations that might assist us to survive and thrive. When we recognise a familiar situation our brain executes pre-learned actions swiftly and effortlessly. For example, when you recognise a cup of tea in front of you and you are feeling thirsty, your brain effortlessly organises the subtle motor actions required to pick up the cup, bring it to your lips and pour the tea into your mouth. Pre-learned routines can be complex and highly interactive with your environment. For example, have you ever had the experience of driving on a familiar route and when you arrived at your destination you had no recollection of how you got there? If so, it's more than likely that the management of your journey was controlled by a set of learned AUTOPILOT brain processes, like recognising the roads down which you drove and operating the steering wheel, accelerator, brakes, clutch and gear shift of your car. Why would your brain operate in this way? AUTOMATIC brain processes use far less energy than effortful, controlled JUDGE ones.

However, with AUTOMATIC brain processes, we can default to patterns of thinking which sometimes can lead us to inappropriate actions. These automatic patterns of thinking can take the form of assumptions or mindsets about people or situations. For example:

- I assume that if a colleague looks and sounds like they don't understand a problem then they don't have the capacity to work it out
- You have to be an expert already to solve a complex problem or meet a complex challenge
- I assume a more senior person must always be expert, make good decisions and not make mistakes otherwise I can't respect them
- I assume that if a colleague only gives critical feedback they see nothing valuable in my work
- I assume that if a colleague finds no fault with my work there aren't ways in which I could improve it myself

Exercise 2 – Automatic patterns of thinking

Here's another quick exercise that Stella did which you can do. Briefly describe a recent occasion when you defaulted to an automatic pattern of thinking (an assumption or mindset) that, with hindsight, you recognise as wrong. When you've written your response park it again for now.

Threat or opportunity?

One of the great human strengths is our inclination and ability to predict the future so that we can survive and thrive in it. When we are not trying to solve particular problems, like how to choose our next mobile device or multiply two numbers, much of our mental activity defaults to making sense of our relationships. We try to make sense both of our relationships with others and the relationships between others. Why would our brains operate in this way? Much of the success of the human species can be put down to its ability to live and work in groups. Evolving a brain that can track multiple relationships is an essential component of that success.

How do our brains track these multiple relationships? In chapter 2 we explored the different purposes of the *narrative neural network* and the *direct experience neural network* in the human brain. To summarise, the *narrative neural network* creates narratives about our own and other people's histories while the *direct experience neural network* operates when we experience new information coming into our senses in real time both from external and internal sources. Norman Farb[3] noticed that the two networks are inversely correlated. In plain English, while I am preoccupied making up stories about how you and I either do or don't get along, I become less good at noticing what's going on around me and my emotional reaction in response. Why might this matter in a leadership context?

Let's imagine you and I are about to meet to discuss a work project that I am leading. I start to create a narrative to help me to predict how the meeting will go. Let's contrast two possible, very different narratives:

Narrative A:

I reflect that the last couple of times we met, I stated some views on the work project and you listened and acknowledged my point of view. You told me where you agreed with me and where you disagreed and why. We discussed the merits of each other's arguments and while we didn't agree on everything we agreed enough things to form a plan of action. Since then we've both done what we said we would do. My conclusion is that you are someone with whom I can do business.

Narrative B:

I reflect that the last couple of times we met, I stated some views on the work project and you didn't listen or acknowledge my point of view. You told me your point of view but did not invite me to comment on it. We didn't agree any actions from the meetings and we each went off and did whatever we wanted without reference to the other. My conclusion is that you are not someone with whom I can do business.

Farb's research suggests that if I now enter our next meeting holding either of the above narratives very strongly, I will tend only to notice your words, tones of voice and body language that validate the narrative I am already holding.

However, if I can turn down my *narrative neural network* in the conversation I can:

- Stop looking only for the evidence to validate my narrative
- Keep a more open mind

If I can turn up my *direct experience neural network* I can be aware of:

- The full range of your words, tones of voice and body language
- My own emotional reactions to what you are saying/doing

So why might that matter?

- If I am focused on your words, voice and body language and don't fit them to my pre-existing narrative I can become curious about and explore your behaviour from your perspective
- If I am aware of my emotional reactions to what you say and do I can control them and prevent them controlling me

So what?

I am now ready to do some high quality JUDGE thinking. In a world where more and more business challenges are complex in nature, I need to create and share a greater depth of understanding in order to lead effectively.

Exercise 3 - *Exploring different narratives in order to integrate them*

Here's an exercise which you could try with a colleague with whom you generally get along OK but with whom you recently had a conversation that either of you think somehow went wrong. You may be thinking of the conversation or situation that you started to consider in exercises 1 or 2. Your explicit purpose here is to help both you and your colleague to have a better conversation. Now, I imagine that when you anticipate doing this first bit of the exercise you may feel uncomfortable or awkward so if it helps, just practice in your head what you will say before you say it.

Explain to your colleague that you appreciate having good conversations with them (may be cite an example), that you have a hunch that the last conversation (about x) between the two of you didn't go so well and that now you'd like to put that right and have a better conversation with them. Ask your colleague what they think about that and simply play back their response without your evaluation or judgement. If they're not ready to have a new conversation with you, agree a time and place when they will be ready. If they launch in to the content of your last conversation, say that you'd really like to hear what they have to say and that first you'd like to explain a different way of having a conversation with them that you hope will produce better outcomes for both them and you.

Here are the essential ground rules for the conversation to which you personally promise to adhere. Invite them to do the same:

- Take turns to speak without interruption
- Talking about feelings is OK
- The intent of either person speaking throughout is to improve this relationship

When you are both happy to follow these ground rules then do the exercise. If your relationship with this person is OK I would predict that they would agree readily even if they seem a little surprised by your invitation to make conversation ground rules so explicit. If your relationship is not OK, I would expect that they would struggle to consider let alone agree to these ground rules. If that's the case, invite them in a genuinely friendly manner to do the exercise with you any way. They may just take the plunge. If you're worried about coming across as patronising or just weird, then say "I know that what I'm suggesting might seem a bit patronising or weird, but I genuinely want to have a better conversation with you and I believe that using these ground rules could really help us to do that."

Here is the exercise:

Each of you writes down their recollections of the meeting or telephone conversation that went wrong.

Now take it in turns to describe the meeting/conversation. When you are listening and observing note...

1. Key words, tone of voice and body language signals of your partner who is talking
2. Positive or negative emotions you personally feel as they speak
3. What you infer from what they say

When they have finished speaking immediately feed back all of the above to them. Test your understanding of their behaviour and your inferences with them.

When you have both taken turns to describe your recollections of the meeting or telephone conversation, discuss the following items while still adhering to the ground rules:

- What similarities are there between your narratives?
- What's different?
- Which parts of your colleague's narrative would you like to explore?
- Which parts might you be prepared to add to your own narrative?

- Which parts of your narrative would your colleague like to explore?
- Which parts might your colleague be prepared to add to their own narrative?

Identifying and regulating emotions

In the process of exploring someone else's narrative about a contentious situation or issue, we might easily be triggered into an unwanted emotion that might then motivate us to words or actions that we later regret. Most of us have some skill and ability in recognising our emotions. However, my experiences as a coach and trainer lead me to believe that most of us live our lives with an at best patchy and at worst under-developed awareness of what we are feeling moment to moment and how it is motivating our words and actions. If you are sceptical about that last statement let me invite you to generate your own anecdotal evidence in support of it. Recall a recent situation at work when your stress levels spiked. I imagine that in the preceding seconds or minutes you felt relatively calm and in control. Then something happened and you shifted to feeling mentally agitated and temporarily out of control. I imagine that you then said or did something almost automatically and without much consideration to make the mental agitation and out of control feeling go away. I imagine that ten minutes, or an hour or a day later when you ruminated on the incident you thought of a much more productive thing you could have said or done in the situation. I believe we have the potential to become much better at identifying precisely what we are feeling and why. I also believe it takes practice, practice, practice. Here's a method you could try and practice.

Recognise it

What emotion am I feeling in this situation or conversation? Fear, anger, disgust, sadness, surprise, lust, joy etc.?

Be curious about it

What triggered this emotion in me? Why am I feeling it? What assumptions am I making about the situation and the people in it, including myself, in order to make sense of it all? What narrative have I created? How could that narrative be different?

Accept it without judgement on self or others

It's a feeling and not reality. It's a bunch of neural networks buzzing in your head that somehow has been stimulated and is producing a particular sensation that will pass. It's OK to feel it because your brain is configured that way!

Let it go if you don't want it

Can you imagine the feeling getting smaller, weaker, less distinct or receding to nothing? Can you look at it from the perspective of a dispassionate observer?

Encourage it if you do want it

Can you imagine it getting larger, stronger, more distinct or approaching?

How do we know this kind of introspection works? How do we know that it can make a difference to what you subsequently say and do in a situation or conversation? Here's the neuroscience[4]:

1. The part of the brain called the amygdala is central to organising the brain's appreciation of and response to emotion, especially fear
2. The right ventrolateral pre-frontal cortex (RVLPFC for short!) acts like the brain's emotional 'braking system' and is responsible for our thinking when we reappraise a situation or actively take a different perspective
3. Amygdala activity decreases when RVLPFC activity increases. There is a clear inverse correlation of activity.

In plain English, when we deliberately reappraise a situation or take a different perspective we reduce our experience of negative emotion. Being mindful of our emotions in the moment makes us take a different perspective on what's happening and our place in it.

Exercise 4 – Identifying and regulating emotions

Revisit your recollections of a meeting or telephone conversation with a colleague that went badly (exercise 3). As you work through this new exercise try and think of yourself as a detective simply trying to uncover what happened.

Recognise it – What was your predominant emotion? Spend some time recalling this accurately but at the same time try not to get caught up in it so it overwhelmes you and you lose your objectivity

Be curious about it – What triggered this emotion in you? What was it the other person said or did? What thought in your own head triggered the emotion? For example 'Here we go again, they never listen…' or , 'I'm not allowed to say what I want…', 'I'm not good enough…'

Accept it without judgement on self or others – Write down 'My (emotion you were feeling) is not reality. It just felt that way at the time.'

Finally, if you were to have the conversation again, what would you want to say or do that was significantly more positive for both parties?

Now do this whole exercise again but this time while thinking of a meeting or telephone conversation with a colleague that went well. Only this time:

Accept it with a positive judgement on self or others – Write down 'My (emotion you were feeling) is a positive emotion that I want more of.' What will you do or say to get more of it?

Empathising to influence better

Stella asked me a very obvious question "Why on earth would I want to empathise with someone with a 'difficult' personality?!" And my answer was "To stop feeling difficult with them, move the conversation on or influence them." This would indeed be a powerful reappraisal.

What is empathising? It is thinking from another's perspective plus simulating analogous emotional responses to theirs. In other words both thinking and feeling from their perspective. Matt Lieberman describes how we have the neural architecture to do this[5]. He describes what's happening in our brain when we experience empathy. There is:

- Heightened activity in the 'mentalizing' or 'mindreading' neural network – dorsomedial prefrontal cortex (DMPFC) + temporoparietal junction (TPJ)
- Heightened activity in the septal area rich in oxytocin receptors. Oxytocin mitigates fear responses and promotes bonding

There is a potential virtuous circle here concerning how best to deal with 'difficult' personalities. If we can empathise with a 'difficult' person and see matters from a different perspective, the perspective taking will regulate any negative emotions we are feeling (RVLPFC 'controls' amygdala). If we can regulate any negative emotions we might be feeling towards a 'difficult' person, we may find it easier to empathise with them and see their perspective.

How can empathising help us to influence better? On the face of it this looks contradictory. If we truly empathise with another person who hitherto has held a different opinion or perspective from us, then surely we will cease to hold our own perspective and simply agree with them? I think not. One of the features of JUDGE thinking is the ability to hold different sets of information, different views or perspectives in mind long enough to make meaningful comparisons, evaluate them and come to new, sometimes more complex and subtle judgements. Empathising allows us to understand someone else's narrative and interrogate that narrative to discover on what data it is based. We are then in a position to compare our narrative with theirs – to recognise and explicitly acknowledge the similarities and the differences. We now have the opportunity to integrate those narratives into a new one, which both parties have a hand in creating and to which both parties are therefore more likely to commit. If this sounds a bit theoretical the following short conversation demonstrates just how practical this process can be.

Stella: "Look Michael, my ideas will reduce costs on this project significantly."

Michael: "But Stella, I came to this meeting to discuss ideas for increasing the quality of the product. It's really important to me."

Stella: "OK, so tell me your ideas for increasing quality and let's see how they can work with my ideas to reduce costs."

Michael: "But hang on, your ideas for reducing costs are surely going to be the opposite of my ideas for increasing quality."

Stella: "Are they? We don't know yet that they are mutually exclusive. We're just assuming that's the case. Why don't we explore them?"

Michael: "OK. Well one idea I have is to publish a lot more of the product on line. More and more customers want us to reduce the amount that we print on paper. The customer surveys are showing that they are judging the quality of our product increasingly on the environmental impact it has and they want us to print less in hard copy. It's so important for some customers that they are bad mouthing us around the industry for not paying more attention to it."

Stella: "I can see how worrying that is for you and now that you've told me it bothers me too. I also think it's a great idea to reduce the amount that we print on paper because that will also reduce those costs, which is my concern. How can we ensure that the costs of publishing more on line are not greater than any savings on reduced printing on paper?"

Through empathising Stella has focused their conversation on finding a way forward to meet both her and Michael's needs. Empathising encourages us to understand what others see as the persuasive benefits of a proposition. It also encourages us to see their objections to whatever we are proposing and think how we might deal with those objections.

Exercise 5 – Social and self awareness in conversations and meetings

Here's an exercise from chapter 2 on increasing self and social awareness that also works in this chapter. If you've already done this exercise reread your answer or do it again but using a different example. It can help to reinforce your learning.

Strike up a conversation with a colleague, friend or family member to discuss something that's really important to them.

As the conversation progresses see if you can do the following?

- Make your sole purpose for this conversation to understand their perspective or viewpoint and maintain that purpose throughout
- Focus your attention exclusively on the messages being given by them – both verbal and non-verbal
- Keep the conversation focused on what they are experiencing at this moment in time
- Do not allow thoughts of other tasks you need to do to crowd out your thinking about their experience
- Acknowledge your own responses to what they are saying and the way they say it including any feelings you may have of discomfort and awkwardness, excitement or joy
- Do this in a way that is merely reporting on your responses without judgement either on yourself or on the other person
- Vocalise your responses at appropriate moments in the conversation without interrupting their flow

Hmmm...... it can be a pretty tall order to do all that!

Debrief:

1. When the conversation is over give yourself a mark out of 10 for how well you demonstrated each of the above (1=low, 10=high). (Yes, you now have permission to judge your performance but not your self!)
2. Where you gave yourself less than 8, see if you can identify what either happened in the conversation or in your head that took you off track and write it down. Become conscious of it. For example, was there a particular word or phrase, tone of voice or action that the other person used that produced a particular emotional response in you or provoked a familiar pattern of thinking in you? Was there something you intentionally or unintentionally said or did that you noticed had produced a particular emotional response in them? If it helps write it down.
3. Remind yourself of your observations before you have the next conversation with a colleague, friend or family member to discuss something that's really important to them.

Seeking common ground before exploring differences

Stella wondered whether I was recommending seeking common ground before exploring differences as some sort of moral axiom - as simply "the right thing to do". I replied "No" and that I was being far more pragmatic. I am recommending it because it produces a different outcome from doing things the other way around, namely exploring differences before seeking common ground. Try this next exercise and see what happens.

Exercise 6 – Actively seeking common ground first

In your next conversation when the other person says something with which you disagree, deliberately look for something you can agree with and mention it first. Notice how the other person responds. Do this before stating where you disagree. Throughout the conversation try and keep to the rule of seeking common ground first and exploring differences second. Notice what difference it makes to the conversation, in particular the outcome. Examine why you think it works.

What happened when Stella did the exercises?

Here's how Stella worked through the exercises and the insights at which she arrived.

Exercise 1 – Triggered feelings

Briefly describe a recent occasion when you were triggered into a feeling that motivated you to an action which, with hindsight, was inappropriate or that you later regretted.

Stella: Last week I attended a senior management team meeting. One of the items on the agenda concerned a project to outsource software maintenance and management to an external contractor. You could tell that Colin the CE had an impression from somewhere that implementation of the project was behind schedule and he was digging for some facts. His impression was in fact correct and I knew the facts. Some of my colleagues spoke up straight away and smoothed it over, guiding Colin to the impression that the delays were very minor and it wasn't a problem. I felt that to have challenged their view in the meeting would have been confrontational and disloyal and so I said nothing. Two weeks later when the whole issue blew up in to a full-blown crisis I wished I had said what I had really thought in the meeting. I had wanted to say that delays in implementing the project were likely to cause us some serious problems unless we addressed the situation immediately.

Exercise 2 – Automatic patterns of thinking

Briefly describe a recent occasion when you defaulted to an automatic pattern of thinking that, with hindsight, you recognise as wrong.

Stella: I can build on my recollection concerning the project to outsource software maintenance and management to an external contractor. When the crises came, people dropped everything else to rectify the situation like we always do. Afterwards we carried out a 'post mortem' and as usual became obsessed with finding a different process that would prevent it happening again. My hunch is that we can tinker with process all we like and this sort of situation will still come back to haunt us. The nub of the problem for me does not concern process but the poor working relationships between key departments which, if we're honest, is largely down to a couple of poor relationships between particular department heads. Improving these relationships is where we need to focus our attention for things to improve.

Exercise 3 - Exploring different narratives in order to integrate them

Each of you writes down their recollections of the meeting or telephone conversation that went wrong

Now take it in turns to describe the meeting/conversation. When you are listening and observing note…

1. Key words, tone of voice and body language signals of your partner who is talking
2. Positive or negative emotions you personally feel as they speak
3. What you infer from what they say

When they have finished speaking immediately feed back all of the above to them. Test your understanding of their behaviour and your inferences with them.

When you have both taken turns to describe your recollections of the meeting or telephone conversation, discuss the following items while still adhering to the ground rules:

- What similarities are there between your narratives?
- What's different?
- Which parts of your colleague's narrative would you like to explore?

- Which parts might you be prepared to add to your own narrative?
- Which parts of your narrative would your colleague like to explore?
- Which parts might your colleague be prepared to add to their own narrative?

Stella: I raised my concerns about the poor working relationships between particular department heads with my line manager Katerina. We had a short and unusually irritable exchange before both rushing off to other meetings. I wasn't happy with how things had gone so I caught up with her later and asked for her recollections of our conversation.

She recollected that I had seemed a bit quick to blame the recent crisis on poor relations between two particular department heads. She said she'd felt uncomfortable about that. However, she agreed with me that the poor relationships had indeed contributed to the crisis but that she thought there were valid historical reasons behind the poor relationship. She did not volunteer any more information.

I said to Katerina that I inferred that she was unwilling to shed more light on the relationship. She sighed and said that she was indeed reluctant to discuss it because she felt she might be breaking confidences made with other colleagues but that was the only reason for not telling me more. I appreciated her honesty and thanked her for it.

We noted that we both agreed that there was a poor relationship that was having an adverse impact on the business. We noted Katerina's concern to maintain confidences. I said I was curious to explore what she thought we could do about the situation and after some thought she gave me her ideas. I acknowledged them and asked if she wanted to hear my ideas and she said 'yes', heard me out and questioned me to understand me better. I was prepared to add her need to maintain confidences in a delicate situation to my narrative and she was prepared to add my desire to find a solution to the problem to her narrative.

Exercise 4 – Identifying and regulating emotions

Revisit your recollections of a meeting or telephone conversation with a colleague that went badly. As you work through this exercise try and think of yourself as a detective simply trying to uncover what happened.

Recognise it – What was your predominant emotion? Spend some time recalling this accurately but at the same time try not to get caught up in it so it overwhelmes you and you lose your objectivity

Be curious about it – What triggered this emotion in you? What was it the other person said or did? What thought in your own head triggered the emotion? For example 'Here we go again, they never listen…' or , 'I'm not good enough…'

Accept it without judgement on self or others – Write down 'My (emotion you were feeling) is not reality. It just felt that way at the time.'

Finally, if you were to have the conversation again, what would you want to say or do that was significantly more positive for both parties?

Stella: I'm thinking again about the meeting when Colin was digging to find out whether the outsourcing project was on schedule. I recognise now that my predominant emotion was fear. I've seen that aggressive questioning style from Colin before and I've heard him verbally rip people to shreds for less. I guess I was also creating a catastrophe in my own mind about how badly things could go wrong and feeding that fear with one of my default patterns of thinking. Yes, it helps to write down that my fear is not reality. It just felt that way at the time. Colin has his own pressures and fears. He is, in spite of what some might say, human too! Next time I want to speak up. I want to explain in a calm, rational way the seriousness of the situation as I see it but without encouraging people to panic or get defensive. I want to make it clear that being honest about the extent of the problem early is going to help us to find an implement an effective solution.

Exercise 5 – Social and self awareness in conversations and meetings

Strike up a conversation with a colleague, friend or family member to discuss something that's really important to them.

As the conversation progresses see if you can do the following?

- Make your sole purpose for this conversation to understand their perspective or viewpoint and maintain that purpose throughout
- Focus your attention exclusively on the messages being given by them – both verbal and non-verbal
- Keep the conversation focused on what they are experiencing at this moment in time
- Do not allow thoughts of other tasks you need to do to crowd out your thinking about their experience
- Acknowledge your own responses to what they are saying and the way they say it including any feelings you may have of discomfort and awkwardness, excitement or joy
- Do this in a way that is merely reporting on your responses without judgement either on yourself or on the other person
- Vocalise your responses at appropriate moments in the conversation without interrupting their flow

Stella: I found I had five minutes with Colin before a board meeting and took the opportunity to discuss the recent crisis over the outsourcing project. I asked him what he felt about the situation now. He said he was still worried that the crisis would reoccur. He was very honest about what was personally at stake for him if this happened again. He had championed the whole move to outsource non-core work in order to deliver significant operational efficiencies. If outsourcing actually increased operational inefficiencies then the whole policy was dead in the water and his reputation would be badly damaged making him less effective as a CE. As Colin revealed his thoughts I felt really uncomfortable and wanted to break away from the conversation. However, I caught myself feeling this emotion and was immediately curious why I was feeling it. I guess I didn't expect the CE to show this sort of vulnerability but was also curious to know more. So I put my feeling of discomfort to one side and explicitly acknowledged his concerns and asked him to tell me more. After he had shared more, I told Colin my own feelings of discomfort about the situation and my genuine desire for things to improve. He seemed almost relieved that someone else shared his concerns about the situation and also his desire to do something about it.

Exercise 6 – Actively seeking common ground first

In your next conversation when the other person says something with which you disagree, deliberately look for something you can agree with and mention it first. Notice how the other person responds. Do this before stating where you disagree. Throughout the conversation try and keep to the rule of seeking common ground first and exploring differences second. Notice what difference it makes to the conversation, in particular the outcome. Examine why you think it works.

Stella: As the conversation with Colin continued, he wondered whether we needed to look at processes and structures again, since operations just weren't working smoothly enough. My heart sank. Here we go again, I thought, we're focusing on processes and structures when the real problem lies in a couple of key, poor working relationships! But then I thought, OK, at least Colin acknowledges there is a problem in operations. That much we have in common. We just have different perspectives currently on the solution to the problem. So I told Colin I agreed with him on the importance of the problem. Then I said I had a different solution in mind if he was interested. He was now listening attentively. We had a long discussion about our respective solution ideas and while we disagreed frequently during its course, it felt like we were both committed to finding a workable solution and for that reason were more prepared to hear each other's perspective. The conversation had moved forward and by the end of it I felt committed to acting on the items we agreed to do. Colin did what he said he was going to do after our meeting and so did I.

Notes:

1. The Emotional Brain: The Mysterious Underpinnings of Emotional Life, Joseph LeDoux, 1998
2. Making Choices Impairs Subsequent Self-control: A Limited Resource Account of Decision-making, Self-regulation, and Active Initiative, K.D. Vohs, R.F. Baumeister, B.J. Schmeichel, J.M.Twenge, N.M. Nelson and D.M Tice, Journal of Personality and Social Psychology, 94, 5, 883-898, 2008
3. Attentional Modulation of Primary Interoceptive and Exteroceptive Cortices, Norman A. S. Farb, Zindel V. Segal and Adam K. Anderson, Cerebral Cortex, 23(1): 114–126, 2013
4. Putting Feelings into Words: Affect Labelling Disrupts Amygdala Activity to Affective Stimuli, Matthew D. Lieberman, NI Eisenberger, MJ Crockett, S Tom, JH Pfeifer, BM Way, Psychological Science 18, no. 5, 2007. Also, The Common Neural Basis of Exerting Self-Control in Multiple Domains, Jessica R. Cohen and Matthew D. Lieberman, from Self Control in Society, Mind, and Brain, Ran Hassin, Kevin Ochsner, and Yaacov Trope, 2010
5. Empathy: A Social Cognitive Neuroscience Approach, Lian T. Rameson and Matthew D. Lieberman, Social and Personality Psychology Compass 3/1, 94–110, 2009

5. Collaborating in teams

Most of the time leaders don't really 'get' the potential value of teams. I include myself in this judgement! At best we see team colleagues as mere extra hands to execute our existing plans. At worst we see teams as hotbeds of dangerously diverse, uncontrollable thinking and activity. It takes discipline and constant reminders to over come this mindset (AUTOPILOT). Here's a much more enabling mindset that I challenge you to adopt. A team has the potential to do any complex job that can't be done by a computer much, much better than any individual (JUDGE questions AUTOPILOT assumptions). Could you believe it? Or will you pay lip service to it like I did for years and miss out on realising your team's true potential?

In chapter one we heard briefly about Laura, a talented senior operations manager at a leading charity. Laura led a new team merged from two formerly separate teams. There was a clear opportunity for the newly merged team to improve the efficiency and effectiveness of how the organisation made and implemented its funding decisions. This depended on members of the team combining their knowledge, resources and expertise.

Some of the issues which Laura's merged team faced included:

- Team conversations had hitherto focused on differences and there was a need to find common ground

- Some team members were ignorant or suspicious of others' experience, expertise or intent or hadn't shared information

- Some team members' reasoning and intent needed to be more explicit for trust to grow and more honest conversations to happen

- A small group within the wider team tended to dominate conversations and prevent contributions, creativity and commitment from other team members

Over lunch while on a leadership training course Laura told me about the issues she was facing with her team. She was finding the challenge daunting and asked me what she needed to do to lead the team better. In answer, I described some disciplines that I'd observed effective leaders follow. Then I invited Laura to consider how she might apply these disciplines to her own team.

Both effective leaders and effective members of teams at any level of seniority in an organisation practice the following disciplines. They:

1. Create common cause and a sense of belonging
2. Encourage diverse and innovative thinking
3. Facilitate productive discussion and decision making

For better or worse

Viewed through the lens of our brain processes model, here's how our thinking about collaborating in teams could make us lead more effectively.

Think better, lead collaboration in teams better

Brain Processes	Cognitive (Thinking) Purpose: True or false	Affective (Feeling) Purpose: Avoid or approach
Controlled • serial • effortful • evoked deliberately • good introspective access	J U D G E e.g. Encourage team members to share data and different perspectives Facilitate discussion of data so that team members can evaluate and make better judgements and decisions	F R I E N D e.g. Empathise with different perspectives of team members to discover data
Automatic • parallel • effortless • reflexive • poor introspective access	A U T O P I L O T e.g. Encourage tried and tested team processes and norms for behaviour to kick start team effectiveness, but be open to developing or even dumping these as the team develops its own autonomous processes and norms	A N I M A L e.g. Encourage natural easy bonding between team members plus actively encourage bonding between team members who are initially less comfortable with each other

In contrast, here's how our thinking about collaborating in teams could make us lead less effectively.

Think worse, lead collaboration in teams worse

Brain Processes	Cognitive (Thinking) Purpose: True or false	Affective (Feeling) Purpose: Avoid or approach
Controlled • serial • effortful • evoked deliberately • good introspective access	J U D G E e.g. Overload team's ability to think with too much information Over facilitate discussion to the point of repetition or stagnation	F R I E N D e.g. Over-empathise with different perspectives of team members to the point of paralysis
Automatic • parallel • effortless • reflexive • poor introspective access	A U T O P I L O T e.g. Set team processes and norms for behaviour in stone for all time with no prospect of responding to changes in the environment	A N I M A L e.g. Assume that team members who initially hit it off will remain that way without maintaining the relationships. Assume that team members who initially don't hit it off will always stay that way.

Creating common cause

In chapter three we explored how important a sense of purpose is to individual motivation. The same is true for groups of people or teams. However, where there is a team, leaders need to ensure there is a common sense of purpose or a common cause. The most powerful causes that motivate teams to work together are usually pretty broad brush. They are concerned with things like 'making life better for people', 'gaining a life changing experience' or 'living a dream'. These may seem on first inspection to be light years away from the challenges facing most teams in business, but closer inspection reveals some interesting insights. Most teams in business are presented with a challenge or problem that requires some mix of the following – providing better customer service, developing new products or services, introducing or maximising use of technology, changing or maintaining processes, systems or procedures. Think about it. All of these could be reframed as one or more of the broad-brush causes above. The difference is that people commit to ideas like 'making life better for people' much more than ones like 'providing better customer service'. People in general seem to have an optimistic bias and respond well to positive framing[1].

A lot of organisations have a clearly expressed cause. However, a lot of functional or project teams fail to articulate the organisation's cause at the team level. This lies at the heart of many teams not working together as well as they might. Leaders need to get this right to achieve synergy and it is has to be a priority for them.

When leaders create a strong, commonly shared cause with groups of people, they create what psychologists call an 'in-group'. The advantage of in-groups is that individual members are motivated to work hard for each other. Belonging to an in-group is more than a psychological concept. There is increasing evidence from the world of neuroscience that significant neuro-hormonal changes occur when in-group members interact. For example, levels of oxytocin in those interacting tend to rise. Oxytocin reduces fear/anxiety responses between people and facilitates bonding. It stops us seeing others as a threat. It promotes protecting and nurturing behaviours[2]. In males and some females it can also increase aggression towards out-group members. This is a potential threat to team work. Bonding exclusively with one group of people might alienate us from other groups and them from us. So in business it's important to be clear that as individuals we belong to many and variously defined groups or teams. We need to belong to many in-groups. I've worked in businesses where a closely bonded functional team has come to regard other functional teams as competitors. For example, I once belonged to 'a band of sales brothers' who frankly saw the operational and finance teams as the enemy. That mindset undermined the overall performance of the organisation. Similarly, I've seen new project teams define themselves in opposition to the rest of the organisation and either fail the project or, in one case, nearly kill the organisation! There is an increasing awareness that for an organisation really to 'fly', individuals need to bond with other individuals across functions and projects. This kind of bonding is encouraged when individuals' commit to a common cause framed at the business level and a common cause framed at the functional or project team level and when these two causes are entirely congruent.

For example,

Here is the common cause of Laura's organisation:

'We want to achieve major improvements in people's health through funding the most promising research.'

This is entirely congruent with the common cause bonding Laura's functional team, namely:

'To encourage and facilitate high quality applications for research funding and assist applicants with the process in order to help the funding committees to make the best decisions.'

Here's another example of congruence between organisation and team causes:

Organisaton cause:
'Our Institute is committed to assisting members of our profession so that they achieve their potential through gaining the highest possible level of qualification and competence.'

Team cause:
'Our team is committed to providing examination candidates with the smoothest and least stressful experience of the whole professional examinations process.'

Here's an exercise which Laura did with her team to create the common cause and promote team bonding which you could do with either a functional or project team.

Exercise 1 – Creating common cause

1. Ask the people in your team individually to write down:
    ➤ What do you regard as the primary purpose or mission of this team?
    ➤ What personally gets you up in the morning to work for this team?
    (An answer like 'to make money' rarely represents people's real, intrinsic motivators consistently to give of their best for the team. So invite people to think beyond such an answer.)
2. Next, invite each individual to share their thoughts, highlight and explore the commonalities
3. As a group agree, draft and agree a simple form of words which captures the common cause of the team and is motivational with people
4. Check the common cause of the team is entirely congruent with the common cause of the organisation

Encouraging diverse and innovative thinking

The biggest challenges which businesses face today and the ones that potentially provide the greatest rewards tend to be complex in nature. For example, 'how do we shift our services online?' or 'how do we differentiate what we offer from new competition?' We often look to solve complex problems through teamwork. If teamwork is going to out-perform individual work we need to explore questions like 'How can a number of brains interact to produce better results than one brain alone?' 'What are the features of those interactions and what can leaders and team members do to encourage them?'

Complex problem solving requires gathering large amounts of information. It requires evaluating that information, and looking for connections. It requires making meaning from those connections. Brain processes associated with memory and gaining insights are particularly important in complex problem solving.

What do we know about how memory works in the human brain that might be useful here?

Most neuroscientists currently recognise that the human brain has three types of memory - sensory, short-term and long-term[3]. Chalabi, Turner and Delamont summarise this neatly. With sensory memory "…all information received by the senses is stored before being passed to the conscious mind and stored in short-term memory. Sensory memory can store as much information as is received at any one time, but only for about a third of a second. If we do not attend to it, such information does not pass to short-term memory." "Short-term memory lasts only seconds and is a temporary store before information is consolidated into long-term memory. Short-term memory can hold about seven different pieces of information for about twenty seconds (although it can hold on to information for minutes at a time). Chunks of information count as a single piece, regardless of how complex each piece is, provided they can be coded as a concept. For example a hyphenated telephone number is easier to remember than a long string of single digits." "Transferring information from short-term to long-term memory…. requires either a level of emotional or intellectual understanding or a reduction in complexity. This process of transfer is learning and requires the conversion of information from electrical charge to biochemical and physical changes." We can draw the following conclusions from this information:

- Each individual's long-term memory of a specific event (beyond a few minutes) will likely be very different
- The potential power of a group of human brains is greater than just one brain in terms of both breadth, depth and accuracy of information and possible insights to meaning (i.e. super-charged JUDGE thinking!)

For example, imagine the complex problem of evaluating just how well an important business meeting has gone. Imagine a meeting between representatives of a supplier business on the one hand and representatives of a potential customer business on the other. Let's say two people from the supplier business meet with two people from the potential customer organisation. After the meeting, when the two people from the supplier pool their memories of what happened in the meeting it has the potential to be a much richer source of information on what really happened than relying on just one set of memories. Pooling three sets of memories is potentially even richer than relying just on two and so forth. Many brains can provide input of larger amounts of information to the problem solving process.

What do we know about how the human brain gains insights that might also be useful here?

Often the focus of our problem solving is the use of deliberate, conscious search strategies. When we operate the same old conscious search strategies that we have always used, we tend to end up with the same old solutions. That's fine if the same old solutions work but what if they don't and we need to innovate? John Kounios and Mark Beeman's research[4] shows that insight is a sudden comprehension - the 'Aha!' moment - and occurs when a solution to a problem is computed unconsciously and later emerges into awareness suddenly. Insight involves a conceptual reorganisation of the elements of a problem that results in a new, nonobvious interpretation and an innovation. This kind of reorganising of the elements of a problem can be provoked by new information. The observations or perspective of a team colleague in discussion can provide that valuable new information that will provoke the conceptual reorganisation of the elements of a problem and a new insight.

In summary, having more brains working on a problem potentially increases the chance of useful information being attended to, insights gained and innovative solutions generated. (Hence super-charged JUDGE thinking!)

Exercise 2 – Encouraging diverse thinking

Invite your team to bring one, complex problem or challenge for the whole team to consider.

1. Each person individually writes down[5]:
   - Their understanding of the problem
   - How the world would be a better place if the problem were solved
   - What they believe to have caused the problem or likely contributory factors and why
   - What options they see the team has for solving the problem and the benefits and costs of each of those options (including any combinations of options) and finally their recommended actions
2. Working in groups of three, each individual explains their analysis and recommended actions to their colleagues in less than five minutes without interruption. Colleagues can question for clarity but not challenge or critique
3. Each group now reports its commonalities and differences in plenary
4. Everybody listens and writes down information, perspectives or insights that are new to them prompted by what they have just heard
5. Take a break and do something else entirely different for 20-30 minutes
6. Bring the whole team back into new groups of three and each individual expresses any more insights they have had to the problem as a result of a new piece of information provided by somebody else. Each group shares these in plenary for discussion and evaluation

Facilitating productive discussion and decision making

When it comes to complex problem solving there is potentially huge value in a leader facilitating productive rather than destructive group discussion and decision making. But what exactly is a leader's role in ensuring that a team attends to information, gains insights to the problem or challenge at hand and generates innovative solutions? Perhaps the greatest value a good facilitator brings to team problem solving is helping team members to hold different information and perspectives in mind long enough to make meaningful comparisons and evaluations. (Longer than the seconds or at best minutes of one individual's short-term memory.) Put another way, the good facilitator creates the environment for a group of people to put forward their arguments, for those arguments to be examined and evaluated thoroughly on their merits and for participants to synthesise new insights and ideas.

How does this happen? The answer lies in the facilitator explicitly encouraging the use of ground rules by those involved in discussion with the express purpose of making that discussion more productive for all involved. Here the facilitator can turn to the assistance of an expert in the shape of Roger Schwarz who recommends the following ground rules[6]:

1. State views and ask genuine questions
2. Share all relevant information
3. Use specific examples and agree on what important words mean
4. Explain reasoning and intent
5. Focus on interests, not positions
6. Test assumptions and inferences
7. Jointly design next steps
8. Discuss un-discussable issues

Exercise 3 – Facilitating productive discussion and decision making

1. Call a meeting of colleagues to discuss a serious work issue where you know there are currently a number of different, opposing views.
2. Warm up. Invite people to pair up with someone in the room who they know currently holds a different opinion from them on the serious work issue in question. If a participant can't find someone then they join a pair as an observer, with two observers per pair as a maximum.
3. Invite your colleagues consciously to use two ground rules in particular in the conversation they are about to have for up to 20 minutes:

    ➢ Focus on interests, not positions
    ➢ Test assumptions and inferences

4. Each pair now starts a conversation in which each person tries to influence the other while using the ground rules above. The observer notes the use of each of the ground rules with specific examples. At the end of the conversation the observer feeds back their observations and the difference the ground rules made to the progress of the conversation.
5. Now, bring all the team members back together. Invite them to discuss the serious work issue at hand but this time as a whole group and while observing all eight of the ground rules. Invite the group to self-facilitate the discussion but be prepared to step in and actively facilitate yourself if you hear the conversation becoming toxic or going off track because a ground rule is being ignored and needs to be applied to move the conversation forward.

What happened when Laura did the exercises?

Here's how Laura worked through the exercises and the insights at which she arrived.

Exercise 1 – Creating common cause

1. Ask the people in your team individually to write down:
   - What do you regard as the primary purpose or mission of this team?
   - What personally gets you up in the morning to work for this team?
     (An answer like 'to make money' rarely represents people's real, intrinsic motivators consistently to give of their best for the team. So invite people to think beyond such an answer.)
2. Next, invite each individual to share their thoughts, highlight and explore the commonalities
3. As a group agree, draft and agree a simple form of words which captures the common cause of the team and is motivational with people
4. Check the common cause of the team is entirely congruent with the common cause of the organisation

Laura: The team met on an away day and we did this exercise. There was a huge amount of commonality in the responses to the questions:

- *What do you regard as the primary purpose or mission of this team?*
- *What personally gets you up in the morning to work for this team?*

This pleasantly surprised some people. They had not expected team members to share so much common team cause. Individual answers included:

'The work of this team is pivotal in attracting applications for investment in medical research from projects which have the best chance of making significant contributions to improving human health.'

'The scientists who apply for funding are really committed to making improvements in people's health. It's quite humbling to realise how much of their lives they have committed to their research. The least we can do is help them to explain the potential of their projects in a

way which best prepares them for assessment by the funding decision committees.'

'This organisation is very clear about what sort of projects it wants to fund. It's our job to steer applications from those kind of projects towards the assessment committees and steer away those projects that don't fit our investment criteria so that they can seek funding elsewhere.'

Once everyone had shared their thoughts, uninterrupted in plenary, we decided to break into small groups to draft a simple form of words which captured the common cause of the team and which would be motivating for people. Finally, we came back together as one group and went through a number of iterations before agreeing on the final draft of the team cause. Looking from the outside the following words may not appear very exciting or earth shattering but for team members they possessed a lot of meaning.

'To encourage and facilitate high quality applications for medical research funding and assist applicants with the process in order to help the funding committees to make the best decisions.'

Exercise 2 – Encouraging diverse thinking

Invite your team to bring one, complex problem or challenge for the whole team to consider.

1. Each person individually writes down[5]:
    - Their understanding of the problem
    - How the world would be a better place if the problem were solved
    - What they believe to have caused the problem or likely contributory factors and why
    - What options they see the team has for solving the problem and the benefits and costs of each of those options (including any combinations of options) and finally their recommended actions
2. Working in groups of three, each individual explains their analysis and recommended actions to their colleagues in

under five minutes without interruption. Colleagues can question for clarity but not challenge or critique

3. Each group now reports its commonalities and differences in plenary
4. Everybody listens and writes down information, perspectives or insights that are new to them prompted by what they have just heard
5. Take a break and do something else entirely different for 20-30 minutes
6. Bring the whole team back into new groups of three and each individual expresses any more insights they have had to the problem as a result of a new piece of information provided by somebody else. Each group shares these in plenary for discussion and evaluation

Laura: The team brought the following problem for us all to consider:

How do we work more cross-functionally?

When the team members shared their analysis and recommendations it became clear that different team members had different conceptions of what they meant by working 'more cross-functionally'. For example, one sub-group of people meant that they wanted greater access to support at busy times from their colleagues. We teased out in discussion that people in this sub-group had a perception that they were working harder or had more time-consuming tasks than members of other teams. I was able to share evidence that this was not the case. Another sub-group of people understood working 'more cross-functionally' to mean that there was an opportunity to influence others to change their working practices to bring them more in to line with their own preferred ones. I was concerned that this mindset might stifle an evidence-based assessment of the efficacy of different working practices. So I encouraged the group to find out more about how others work and without a positive bias toward their own current practices. A further sub-group understood working 'more cross-functionally' to mean genuinely wanting to compare working practices with the purpose of learning how to be more effective as individuals, as a functional team and across functional teams. With permission of the whole group I chose to focus discussion on this last group's definition of working 'more cross-functionally'.

Most people listened and wrote down information, perspectives or insights that were new to them from what they heard in discussion. Then we took a break. When the whole group gathered into new groups to share insights an interesting thing happened. Some of the groups started to redefine the problem in new ways. Instead of asking 'How do we work more cross-functionally?', one group substituted 'How can we work together more effectively for our stakeholders?'. Another substituted 'What do and will our customers, internal and external, value most from us now and in the future?' This made the discussions more outward looking, bigger picture and more focused on the longer-term.

Exercise 3 – Facilitating productive discussion and decision making

1. Call a meeting of colleagues to discuss a serious work issue where you know there are currently a number of different, opposing views.
2. Warm up. Invite people to pair up with someone in the room who they know currently holds a different opinion from them on the serious work issue in question. If a participant can't find someone then they join a pair as an observer, with two observers per pair as a maximum.
3. Invite your colleagues consciously to use two ground rules in particular in the conversation they are about to have for up to 20 minutes:

   ➢ Focus on interests, not positions
   ➢ Test assumptions and inferences

4. Each pair now starts a conversation in which each person tries to influence the other while using the ground rules above. The observer notes the use of each of the ground rules with specific examples. At the end of the conversation

the observer feeds back their observations and the difference the ground rules made to the progress of the conversation.

5. Now, bring all the team members back together. Invite them to discuss the serious work issue at hand but this time as a whole group and while observing all eight of the ground rules. Invite the group to self-facilitate the discussion but be prepared to step in and actively facilitate yourself if you hear the conversation becoming toxic or going off track because a ground rule is being ignored and needs to be applied to move the conversation forward.

Laura:

1. *We called a meeting of six department heads to discuss what management development we wanted for our new managers and team leaders. We already knew there were a number of different, opposing views. Rob wanted a programme specifically designed for the needs of the managers in his Facilities team. His view was that the challenges that they faced were unique in the organisation. Fiona from Sales and Marketing wanted budget to put a few of her 'rising stars' on a business school programme which she rated and had attended herself 10 years ago. Stefan from Legal wanted an in-house programme focused on encouraging participants from across the organisation to get to know each other and work together better. As the incoming Head of Operations I shared a similar perspective with Stefan. Ed, the outgoing Head of Operations and due to retire shortly, favoured a mentoring scheme of the sort that had benefitted him earlier in his career. James from HR wanted to harness value from management development specialists from outside the organisation who could design and deliver a programme that would be bespoke and yet draw on best practice from across many industries. With all these different positions, it was going to be an interesting meeting!*

2. *I explained the purpose and process of the exercise to my colleagues who agreed to try it, sold on the possibility of having more productive conversations with better outcomes for everybody involved. Who could argue with that?! They*

organised themselves into discussion groups of three people. Two people in each group spent the next 20 minutes in discussion, each one trying to influence the other to support their position while using the ground rules: (1) focus on interests, not positions and (2) test assumptions and inferences. At the end the observer gave feedback on their use. Here's a rough transcript of the conversation I had with Fiona with Ed observing:

Laura: "Fiona, do you want to kick off and describe what sort of development you would like for new managers and team leaders?"

Fiona: "Yes, of course. I guess I'm keen for any sort of development really to stretch and challenge our new managers. I think it needs to be aspirational, about wanting to get on and do better ..... not just about the basics of management which I suspect they already know. Do you know what I mean?'

Laura: "Well, may be...tell me more."

Fiona: "I was thinking of the business school programme I attended. It has academic credibility and the university has a lot of kudos which is important for new managers' CVs..."

Laura: "...But don't you think those programmes are too academic for a new manager? They don't need all that theory and all those modules on strategy and finance or whatever. Surely they just need something very practical on how to get the best from people. Things they can use back at work the next day?"

Fiona: "But if you don't use a respected business school, how do you know the content of a programme is going to be of any practical use?"

Laura: "Well, I think you're wrongly assuming that there aren't any useful programmes or providers of development outside of the universities."

Fiona: "No, I'm not saying that. I just think why not go for the best for our people?"

Laura: "Again, you are assuming that only universities provide the best which I don't agree with..."

Ed: "Can I interrupt here Laura and Fiona? I'm supposed to note down your use of two ground rules for productive conversations, namely (1) focus on interests, not positions and (2) test assumptions and inferences. I hate to tell you this but so far in this discussion I haven't heard any examples of the use of either ground rule from either of you! Would you like to start over?"

Both Laura and Fiona laugh.

Laura: "Yes, of course! Fiona. I think you said that you thought the kudos of having attended a business school programme is important for new managers. Have I got that right?"

Fiona: "Yes."

Laura: "OK, I agree with you that any programme we have needs to have kudos and be credible. We definitely have that in common. Can I ask you something?"

Fiona: "Of course."

Laura: "What leads you to believe that it is specifically a business school programme that new managers want?"

Fiona: "Well, I suppose my personal experience is that I went on a highly reputable business school programme so why wouldn't they want that too?"

Laura: "Have any of our new managers or team leaders specifically requested to go on a business school programme?"

Fiona: "No. Not specifically."

Laura: "And you know that's been my experience too. In fact, I'm quite worried about the fact that none of the new managers or team leaders in operations have asked for any kind of development at all. And I find that curious and faintly depressing."

Fiona: "You know what?! I feel exactly the same way. Isn't it weird?! When I was their age I was pushing to go on any management programme going and when I did I would use the fact that I had been to hustle senior management for my next promotion! Now I'm a senior manager I don't get any of that from my people in sales and marketing. They seem just so weighed down and rushed off their feet with their existing jobs. I think it might have been easier when we were juniors!"

Laura: "May be so!....and while I think about it I wonder whether the only way any programme of development is going to sell itself to new managers is if it focuses on helping them to gain more control over their working lives."

Fiona: "Hmmm, that's interesting. I agree that on the face of it, development for new managers is most likely to appeal if it addresses the issue of gaining more control. That seems like a pretty good hunch to me. Do you have any hard evidence to back it up?"

Laura: "Not really and I agree that it's a hunch. Given that we both agree with that hunch, would it be worth our while checking it out with new managers themselves? What do you think?"

Fiona: "Good idea."

Ed: "Would you like some feedback at this point on your use of the ground rules?"

Fiona and Laura: "Yes please."

Ed:"When you started and were not using the ground rules, the conversation seemed to polarise quite quickly. It seemed quite confrontational and you both quickly became entrenched. Then after you restarted, Laura, you immediately tested whether you had understood correctly that Fiona thought that the kudos of attending a business school programme was important for new managers. Then you pointed out a shared interest with Fiona namely, that you agreed with her that any management development programme would have to have kudos and be credible.

I noticed a bit further in the conversation that Laura you asked Fiona "Have any of our new managers or team leaders specifically requested to go on a business school programme?" Fiona how did you feel about that question? I ask because if I were you I might have felt a bit threatened by it.

Fiona: "Actually, I didn't feel threatened by that question because Laura had already established a powerful common interest with me. She had agreed that any programme we went for would need to have high kudos and credibility and, you know, that's the most important thing for me. So she'd part won me over. So when she asked me that question "Have any of our new managers or team leaders specifically requested to go on a business school programme?", I felt it was easy to say honestly "No. Not specifically." It already felt more like we were on the same side. I was beginning to think she might know of some other highly credible programmes. That's something I'd now like to ask her about."

Ed continued to provide more examples of where Laura and Fiona had used the ground rules. Laura reported to me afterwards that it had helped to hear these specific examples from Ed and how they had impacted the course of the conversation. A few weeks later Laura also reported that the process of noticing shared interests in conversations with others and pointing them out before differences was a skill that benefitted greatly from practice. She also reported that after a while it had almost become an unconscious skill for her in many situations although not all.

3. Here is a rough transcript of the first few minutes of discussion between all six, department heads where they used a variety of the ground rules to make progress:

Laura: "Thank you all for coming to this meeting to discuss what sort of management development we need for our new managers and team leaders. First, as I think I've mentioned to all of you already, we're going to use all eight ground rules to help the discussion and decision making along. Our aim is to have a better quality of discussion and come to a better decision to which we can all commit. Are we all up for that? (Resounding 'Yes' from all present). OK, the aim of this discussion is to decide what sort of programme we want and specifically the purpose and objectives of that programme. We've got an hour for this meeting and if we need more time for discussion we will reconvene at a follow up meeting. As you know we've already had some discussion in smaller groups. Rob, would you like to summarise your discussion so far with Stefan?

Rob: "I would. Stefan and I had what I think they call a free and frank exchange of opinions on the topic at the start of our discussion! But James kept us moving forward by encouraging us to use the ground rules and we did make progress. What we noticed by the end of our conversation was that things which had appeared to be opposites in terms of our respective requirements were not necessarily so. In other words, while we both came to the meeting with different requirements, both could actually be met with a bit of listening and creative thinking. For example, Stefan really wants to use the programme to get new managers from any department to talk more to each other. And he isn't interested in encouraging idle banter! He wants new managers to talk to each other about the main challenges that they face. He wants them to talk openly about how one department's problems can, often unwittingly, be caused by actions in another department. He wants new managers to talk openly about how different departments can work together better to find solutions to those problems. Is that a fair summary Stefan?"

Stefan: "Yes, it is, and I can add to that. Rob's managers face some very particular challenges. Some involve other departments but a great many don't. We agreed that whatever was taught on the programme there needed to be an emphasis that learning should be done in the context of those real work problems or challenges that individual participants face whether they are peculiar to their own department or involve other departments. So we agreed that new managers should come to any training with specific challenges in mind to which they could apply their learning."

Fiona: "I agree with you that we want participants to bring their real challenges to the training. I'm also keen for my managers to gain ideas and tips from people with experience from the wider world of business. I think that sparks innovative approaches to problem solving.

Laura: "I agree Fiona that we want to see innovative approaches to problem solving. I'm inferring from what you say that you expect innovative approaches to come from outside the organisation?"

Fiona: "Well, I think we're pretty bad at innovating in this organisation."

Ed: "I agree with you Fiona that we could be a lot better. But I'm inferring Laura that you see innovation as coming from both inside or outside the organisation? Have I got that right?"

Laura: "Yes."

Ed: "What's your evidence?"

Laura: "Well it's only anecdotal from our own department but, for example, last year when we were required by the business to make significant budget savings, one of the best ideas we had to drive improvements in operational processes came from within the department. One of our staff had got so fed up with an existing process that she sat down with end users and asked what they really wanted and then redesigned the whole process to meet the users' needs better. This was a great wake up call for the rest of the department and over the next six months we saw all sorts of initiatives where people were redesigning their processes with their users."

James: "May be I can help here with another example. When we were thinking of reviving and improving the mentoring system, I did quite a lot research into the value of mentoring. Those organisations that had successful mentoring schemes reported that one of the benefits was indeed an increase in innovation. Good mentors from within the organisation were encouraging their mentees to look at problems or challenges in new ways. Interestingly, mentoring schemes worked even better when they were allied with management development that introduced best practice from other sectors and industries."

Laura: "OK, we seem to agree that any development for our managers needs to encourage innovation? Have I got that right?"

All: "Yes"

Laura: "...and we have two views, which are not mutually exclusive, that the sources of innovation can come from both outside and inside an organisation? Have I got that right?"

All: "Yes"

We'll leave the discussion here but I hope you can already see how applying the ground rules for productive conversations was impacting the positivity, clarity and productivity of the discussion.

Notes:

1. Thinking Fast and Slow, Daniel Kahneman, 2011
2. Social Effects of Oxytocin in Humans: Context and Person Matter, Jennifer A. Bartz, Jamil Zaki, Niall Bolger and Kevin N. Ochsner, Trends in Cognitive Science, 15, 7, 2011
3. The Brain: A Beginner's Guide, Ammar Al-Chalabi, Martin R. Turner, R. Shane Delamont, 2006
4. The Aha! Moment: The Cognitive Neuroscience of Insight, John Kounios and Mark Beeman, Current Directions in Psychological Science, 18, 4, 210-216, 2009
5. The Tao of Coaching, Max Landsberg, 1996
6. The Skilled Facilitator, Roger Schwarz, 2002

Acknowledgements:

First, I would like to thank my wife Sue for supporting me in writing this book and in particular for acting as an invaluable sounding board for early drafts. I would also like to thank my Dad for pointing out some errors in grammar.

I would like to thank Manchester Central Library and in particular The Woolfson Reading Room, and Manchester University and in particular the John Rylands Library for providing locations in which I could concentrate and write much of this book.

Finally, I would also like to thank the consultancy MaST International, which has provided me with so many opportunities to learn about leadership and team development over more than a decade and continues to do so. May there always be wind in your sails, ladies and gentlemen!

63445597R00082

Made in the USA
Charleston, SC
05 November 2016